SONGS FROM THE
SILENT PASSAGE

Songs from the Silent Passage

© 2020 by The Chrysostom Society

Published by
Rabbit Room Press
3321 Stephens Hill Lane
Nashville, Tennessee 37013
info@rabbitroom.com

Cover design by Chris Tobias
Cover illustration © 2020 by Stephen Crotts

ISBN 9781951872069

Printed in the United States of America

SONGS
FROM THE
SILENT PASSAGE

THE WRITINGS OF
WALTER WANGERIN, JR.

By members of the Chrysostom Society

MATTHEW DICKERSON

DIANE GLANCY

EUGENE PETERSON

JAMES CALVIN SCHAAP

LUCI SHAW

JOHN WILSON

PHILIP YANCEY

And guest contributor SARA R. DANGER

Edited by
MATTHEW DICKERSON and ANNE M. DOE OVERSTREET

CONTENTS

Introduction

John Wilson

THE BEST PLACE TO START this book is at the end, with Philip Yancey's magnificent afterword, which begins with a concise appreciation of the richly various essays gathered here, each taken in turn, and moves from there to reflections on Walter Wangerin's work, the arc of his writing life, and the man himself, based on decades of close friendship and correspondence. His afterword orients the reader for the volume as a whole.

There is one point made in the afterword I want to take up, because it bears on our sense of Wangerin in relation to his contemporaries and near contemporaries. "Walt knew he was swimming against the tide," Yancey writes. "He spoke of the 'cool pragmatism' of modern literary taste. . . . He sought instead to draw the reader into another world, a suspension of disbelief carried more by music and lyricism than by sense or reason." Wangerin himself has often propounded this perspective (see for example, "The Art of Story," an interview with Wangerin conducted by Jeanette Hardage and published in issue number 19 [2002] of the *Mars Hill Review*). We should take this stance—that of a writer self-consciously set apart from his contemporaries—with a grain of salt. It's the sort of myth artists, in all sincerity, invent to sustain their enterprises.

A couple of years ago, while looking for something else, I stumbled on a list of American fiction writers born in the 1940s, listed by year. I went through the list, jotting on the back of an envelope the names of those writers who particularly interested me—some of them writers I love, others I read because they compel my attention. I was pleased when I was done to see that there were ten altogether. They are, in alphabetical order, Peter Abrahams (aka Spencer Quinn), Ann Beattie, Octavia E. Butler, Samuel R. Delany, William Gibson, Diane Glancy, Stephen King, Marilynne Robinson, Walter Wangerin Jr., and Larry Woiwode.

I still have that envelope. I don't claim oracular authority for it. Ask another five readers to go through the same document and each of them would come up with another list of fiction writers, perhaps slightly overlapping with mine, perhaps not overlapping at all, and which may or may not include Wangerin. (But then, "fiction writer" doesn't begin to apprehend the wild profusion of books Wangerin has written.) But never mind. I think you'll concede that my list includes a range of writers in some respects quite various whose collective readership is enormous, writers who have been honored with all manner of acclaim. And surely you'll acknowledge that "cool pragmatism" isn't by and large their ground note.

And who knows what patterns will stand out to readers fifty years hence as they sift through what's survived from roughly 1970 to 2020? Nevertheless, let me make bold to claim that, just as readers of Emily Wilson's recent translation of the *Odyssey* are experiencing that poem in a way Homer's contemporaries could never have foreseen, whatever the "literature of our time" looks like to our counterparts in 2075, say, some of them will still be reading Wangerin, seeing in him some of what we see today—some of what is luminous in these essays—but also reading him in ways that we couldn't now imagine.

Chauntecleer and the Pastoral Imagination

Eugene Peterson

The Book of the Dun Cow (1978)

The Book of Sorrows (1985)

The Third Book of the Dun Cow: Peace at the Last (2013)

READING THE DUN COW NOVELS turned out to be, in retrospect, a significant event in the shaping of my pastoral imagination. After I was ordained and admitted to the company of pastors, I expected to be in conversation with men and women who would be colleagues attentive to the nature of congregation: the beauty of holiness, the care of souls, the craft of preaching. What I found was a "company of shopkeepers," preoccupied with shopkeepers' concerns: how to keep the customers happy, how to lure customers away from the competitors down the street, how to package the goods so that the customers would lay out more money. I began to look around for congenial companions. The search was not easy, but help came in the form of a novel, *The Book of the Dun Cow*, written by Walter Wangerin Jr. It embedded itself in my imagination and along with his subsequent books has continued for nearly forty years to clarify and deepen my understanding and practice of the life of a pastor.

What I am writing here is not so much about Wangerin as such but about his considerable influence on my life as a pastor and writer.

GEOFFREY CHAUCER AND WALTER WANGERIN JR.

One of my assignments as a student at Seattle Pacific University in my final year (1954) was to write a weekly opinion column for *The Falcon*, our student newspaper. In one issue my opening sentence was, "This is the dullest thing since calculus and Chaucer . . ." (I no longer remember "the thing" that I was referring to). I soon got a call from my English professor, who was also advisor to the paper, asking me to come and see her. I showed up and she asked me, "Eugene, have you ever read Chaucer?" I confessed that I had not. She followed up with, "And I assume you know nothing about calculus either?" I admitted my ignorance. Without further comment she turned around, reached for Chaucer's *Canterbury Tales*, and as she handed it to me, said, quite severely it seemed to me, "Read this, and don't come back until you have read the whole thing."

She was my favorite professor and had always treated me kindly, but by the tone of her voice, I knew I was in trouble. I showed up four days later (it's a long book) thoroughly chagrined, for those four days had put me in the company of twenty-nine pilgrims on their way to Canterbury who amused themselves on their journey by telling stories—of adventures and trials, some bawdy and some charming, some of moral philosophical reflection, some of tragedy and some of romance. Twenty-three of the pilgrims told stories and only one out of the twenty-three was dull. By this time, her severity had been replaced by her customary kindness.

In the years that followed, whenever she read a poem or essay that I had written for a periodical, she wrote a note of appreciation that kept our friendship up-to-date. I also learned from others that while teaching her writing course she sometimes would drop my part in the Chaucer incident into the classroom conversation.

Several years later, as a newly ordained pastor in the Presbyterian Church (UPCUSA), I was given an assignment to develop a new congregation near a small town in Maryland (Bel Air) that was fast becoming a suburb of Baltimore. I was pleased to be asked and, ill-equipped as I was, accompanied by my wife and two-year-old firstborn, embraced my new employment with enthusiasm.

There was a burgeoning interest in the church in those years, with experts offering seminars and books exploring the dynamics and procedures for approaching a "generation that knew not Joseph" to get them to listen to the story of Jesus and become part of the body of Christ.

It was the early sixties, the Decade of the Death of God. Church attendance was plummeting. Anxiety—among some approaching something more like hysteria—was widespread as the influence of the Christian church seemed to be swiftly eroding while secular humanism was replacing what many had assumed, probably mistakenly, was a "Christian Nation." Innovations were proposed, desperate applications of tourniquets to staunch the flow of blood from the body of Christ. Churches were modified or designed so they didn't look like churches. The "church growth" movement got most of the headlines—megachurches that seemed to some of us to be mostly "mega" and very little "church."

Meanwhile the primary reaction of the established, so-called mainline churches in response to the challenge was to initiate strategies for developing new congregations. My denomination was energetically recruiting pastors to implement this particular strategy. I counted myself fortunate to be asked to be in on something fresh and new, challenging and demanding, but still "church." I understood that my task was to implement a gathering of men and women who would sit still and be quiet long enough to become aware of God's word and presence in the neighborhood in addition to attending to their own souls.

In anticipation of the population growth in the area, my denomination had purchased six acres of farmland two miles from the existing Presbyterian Church, an historic colonial congregation located in the center of the town but landlocked with no room for expansion. It was an ageing but still vigorous body of Christ, so instead of relocating the church (to "where the people are"), a frequently employed strategy in those years, they requested the denomination develop another congregation.

I was aware, of course, of the advice being handed down by the growing cadre of experts who were telling men and women like me how to counteract the demise of the church by replacing it with something "relevant" to this new post-modern, post-church generation. I attended occasional seminars that seemed promising and read the current books that contained the latest wisdom. But a day came when I read this sentence, written by one of the acclaimed promoters of church renewal: "The size of your parking lot will have a lot more to do with the success of your church than any text you will preach." That sentence raised a red flag. More and more I sensed that I was being encouraged to develop public relations skills borrowed almost verbatim from the world of business. None of these "mentors" seemed to have anything but a cursory interest in theology or people. Theirs was a mindset obsessed with statistics, programs, and demographics. I found myself immersed in a depersonalized world with no relationships.

—◦◦◦—

That's when I picked up and started reading Walt Wangerin's novel *The Book of the Dun Cow* and overnight recovered what I would now name a "pastoral imagination." I say "recovered" because I had already begun to develop a sense of coherence with congregation and worship, with people and God in the place and circumstances that had been given to me, a place where I would cultivate a sense of the holy in the ordinary.

Chaucer and Wangerin entered my story and replaced the experts on relevance that had been boring me to death.

—◦◦◦—

Geoffrey Chaucer (d. 1400), a leading poet in pre-Reformation England, in his most famous poem creates a story about finding himself at an inn as he prepared to set out on a pilgrimage to Canterbury, a cathedral town and popular destination for pilgrims in those days. By chance, he found himself in the company of twenty-nine pilgrims gathered at the Tabard Inn who were also preparing to set out on the pilgrimage. He talked with them, got to know them, and suggested that they travel together and tell stories along the way to lighten the journey. They agreed. The result is the *Canterbury Tales*.

A knight leads off the storytelling, followed in no particular order by the other pilgrims. Some stories are amusing, some overtly religious, some bawdy, some wise and learned, with only one that I recall as excessively boring. Twenty-four stories told by pilgrims on their way to Canterbury.

Now, twenty years later, as I began reading a story about the Dun Cow, I recognized a name I had first encountered in Chaucer's *Tales*—Chauntecleer, a rooster with a coop of hens under his care. I couldn't miss it; it was in the first sentence of the novel I was now reading. The name occurs in Chaucer's "The Nun's Priest's Tale," which also includes two other names used in Wangerin's novel—Chauntecleer's "winsome" wife, Pertelote, and Lord Russell Fox, who talks too much.

Without Chaucer and Professor McAllister's admonition to read him—a timely rescue from my callow ignorance—I would never have recognized that Walt Wangerin's Dun Cow novels were set in a pilgrimage context and written from a pastor/congregational perspective.

THE STORY

As I began *The Book of the Dun Cow*, I had no idea what I would be reading. The author was a new acquaintance and I wanted to get to know his writing. I knew that he had been a Lutheran pastor for fifteen years in a small

Afro-American congregation in Evansville, Indiana. I also knew that he had once kept chickens. (I don't remember how I learned this, but knowing it served to give important texture to the novel.)

By the time I had read the first page, I knew that this was a story that concerned itself with something at the heart of what I was doing vocationally, working with a community of people who were on pilgrimage together and had enough interest in the life of faith to make the effort to take the long trip to get there. And it introduced me to the character of a pastor who was learning on the job what the vocation of pastor involved, a pastor who was a pastor who didn't know how to be a pastor but kept at it all the same. For Chauntecleer the Rooster was pastor to thirty hens in a coop.

As I continued reading, I realized how much I needed a new, authentically pastoral/congregational voice in my life. The church renewal movement had saturated me with clichés and charts and sociological abstractions. But Wangerin's book was an allegory using animals for people, a bestiary. Now I had a story that provided me with a pastor/congregation that was far more interesting and convincing than the secular values and flow charts that were sucking all the juice out of what had been so attractive to me when I started out in this pastor life.

Chauntecleer the Rooster is the lead character in the story I was about to read, the pastor to a coop of thirty hens for whom he provides a sense of belonging in an orderly creation. The most conspicuous way in which he does this is by crowing—"In all the land he had no peer." The seven standard "canonical crows" (lauds, prime, terce, sext, nones, vespers, compline) give shape to the hours of the day. They provide a sense of security, orderliness, well-being. Chauntecleer is a pastor; his crows are either sermons or prayers. There were also "occasional crows" to suit all moods and feelings—grief and celebration, despair and well-being, discouragement and praise. The hens are Chauntecleer's congregation, a coop, not on pilgrimage like Chaucer's pilgrims, but still finding their way with others to a life for whom God is a destination. Through the crowing of the rooster they know they are cared for, that they fit into something greater than themselves, although they would be hard put to say what it is.

———

There were thousands of animals on the earth in those days, but not one was aware of the darkness deep in the guts of the earth under the oceans and continents. This evil was no vague principle or abstraction, but hideously personified: His name was Wyrm. He had the shape of a serpent, damned by God to dwell under the earth. He was

> so damnably huge that he could pass once around the earth and then bite his own tail ahead of him . . . he

stank fearfully . . . he was angry. And he hated, with an intense and abiding hatred, the God who had locked him within the earth. And what put the edge upon his hatred, what made it an everlasting acid inside of him, was the knowledge that God had given the key to his prison in this bottomless pit to a pack of chittering *animals*!

And led by a rooster with thirty hens cooped up in a coop: "Dumb feathers made watchers over Wyrm in chains! It was a wonder. But that's the way it was, because God had chosen it to be that way."

Wyrm, the most comprehensive manifestation of evil, had two accomplices: Cockatrice and the basilisks. Cockatrice, part rooster and part serpent, came into being in a land remote from the land of Chauntecleer, a kind of winged shadow counterpart to Chauntecleer. The basilisks were small serpents, numbering in the thousands—"they made sharp points of their own tails. They sprang from the earth and sailed through the air tail first like darts. They stabbed the hearts of many creatures."

A trinity of evil: Wyrm, Cockatrice, and basilisks.

———

Chauntecleer the Rooster and the coop of hens had been placed on earth to keep evil in check—Keepers and Watchers who served as a protection against an almighty evil, which, if it got past the God-determined bounds, would totally devastate the world and everything in it.

The animals, though, didn't know that they were the Keepers, the Watchers. The Keepers kept Wyrm and his minions in check by responding to Chauntecleer's daily crows. That is all. Simply by worshiping, listening, and responding to their pastor's crows. As Chauntecleer crowed (preached and prayed) and the hens worshiped, the rooster and hens together wove a protective web against the underground evil. Chauntecleer fights for his animals, cares for them, provides for them. There is a blazing exuberance and a fierce goodness in him.

———

Annie Dillard, one of my favorite theologians, wrote, "The basic question of the universe is 'What in the Sam Hill is going on here?'" The bare bones are summarized this way: the "problem of evil" and what Philip Yancey names "The Question that Never Goes Away."

Every religion, every moral system, every parent, every political arrangement that we know of deals with this, usually philosophically. Wangerin tells a story. The Dun Cow novels use Chauntecleer the Rooster, Wyrm the Serpent, and the coop of chickens to invite our participation in the story.

A bad story disguises and suppresses the realities of our lives by providing a temporary escape from our ordinariness. A good story immerses us in everyday realities that show connections, developing comprehensions. An excellent story plunges us into dimensions of our lives we commonly overlook, pulling us into a larger world limned in mysteries.

The Dun Cow novels comprise an excellent story: a comic story, a tragic story, a lively story, a gripping story. But the often-overlooked dimension in our everyday lives that it pulls us into is the abyss of evil—not just the routine pains and bad luck and difficulties that we all manage to absorb—but the abyss of evil. And that does not make for a happy story.

For every hundred writers who set out to work on the problem of evil, explaining and trying to solve it, one or two dare to explore the actual territory. Walter Wangerin Jr. has traveled this baneful country and the Dun Cow novels are his journal. He approaches evil as a mystery to be explored, not as a problem to be explained, and we end up knowing less than ever but realizing more, realizing the repulsive texture of what is so close to us and yet so alien.

"Tell it slant" was Emily Dickinson's counsel for slipping truth past the barriers that we build to protect ourselves from dealing with anything that requires the risk of faith and the rigor of sacrifice. Wangerin's "slant" is a bestiary. His story involves us in a world of animals that talk—a rooster with a coop of hens, a mournful dog, a wonderful weasel, a winsome hen. In this zoo without fence or walls we begin to see the ordering energies of worship and prayer, to realize the gradual but certain presence and operations of the evil that is so thoroughly denied in our American culture, and to discern the penumbra of a pastor and congregation.

The conjunction of the two elements, animals and talk, which never occurs in our experience, provokes recognitions of what is always present but too often overlooked. The animals are enough like humans, talking as they do, to let us see ourselves in them, but are also enough unlike us, being the animals they are, to let us see our unremembered creatureliness, the parts of our lives and of reality that we are too frightened to face or too bored to notice.

The talking animals give the story a childlike quality. But it is not the childlikeness of the nursery. It is the elemental childlikeness commended by Jesus. It gives images to our early perceptions and old memories of innocence and evil, of courage and compassion—the basic stuff of our first years when we were tucked into bed, sung through the disappointments of the day, and protected from the terrors of the night.

—⊗⊗⊗—

Wangerin has created a style of speech for his animals that is just right. They talk the way animals would talk if animals could talk. These are not talking people disguised as animals; these are animals talking, language spoken in a kind of elemental (but not elementary) purity, without our accustomed overlay of convention and gossip. The sentences have sharp edges, not yet blunted by centuries of chatter. Words are used to say, not propagandize or sell. We are close to the roots of language in these animals, not in their grunts and growls, but in directness and simplicity, letting them speak their own meanings and not just using their words as tin-can containers for delivering information. Children sometimes surprise us with this kind of language, courtly in a way that may strike us as almost comic, but what we hear is their sense of dignity, words used with reverence and exactitude.

⚬⚬⚬

All of this is on the earth's surface. In the depths is Wyrm, the huge serpentine evil. As the story develops, an obsession with Wyrm deflects Chauntecleer from the care of his creatures. Increasingly disconsolate in his inability to make all things well, restless within the limits of his responsibilities, Chauntecleer eventually succumbs to the temptation to affect a final solution.

On his own, he sets out to finish off Wyrm, the enormous, subterranean malignity. Returning from his prideful venture, Chauntecleer, without knowing it, brings a yet more odious form of evil into the world of his animals.

Ezra Pound, held by some to be America's most influential poet (but also frequently vilified for his haughty, crackpot solutions to right the world's wrongs), while revising his *Cantos* as he was nearing the end of his life wrote, " . . . I lost my center / Fighting the world." For him, the bottom line, as he defines his final perspective on the purpose of life, is "To be men not destroyers."

This spiritual leader of the animals, Chauntecleer, does what American spiritual leaders typically do—reduces his understanding of evil to something that is manageable as "wrong," and then with jaunty hubris sets out to finish it off for good, shortcutting God. The unintended consequence is the reintroduction of evil in unanticipated ways.

We Americans are not a people who spend much thought or prayer on the subject of evil, and we are unpracticed in dealing with it. From the cradle, we are trained to define whatever is wrong with the world as a problem, to gather the energy and assemble the tools to put an end to it. It is unthinkable that there is some intractable thing, immune to our immense good will and technological prowess. We are used to solving problems. And we are good at it.

But the flurry of our activity in this field obscures our naiveté about evil. A nation of moralizers, we blow the whistle on the faults and infractions of our fellows with the flair of a referee. We are much exercised in dealing with "what's wrong" with the world and church; "what's wrong" is something we can name and about which something can be done. "What's wrong" can be traced to its origin in a person and then confronted, rebuked, and reformed. Even when what is wrong is secularized into ignorance or sickness the same conditions hold true, for it can still be dealt with—helped by education, healed through therapy. Something direct can be done. But evil is something else: malefic, immense, impersonal, beyond management, escaping comprehension. A mystery.

Those of us who have grown up in a world in which a voiceless technology dominates our imaginations tend to discount what we sometimes designate as just words. Words out of a machine. Words isolated from a personal voice, a Babel-like torrent of words separated from anything relational, from a living being—a particular man, a named woman, God revealed in Jesus.

The standard operating procedures practiced outside the orbit of scripture and story and Jesus attempt to get rid of, or at least minimize, whatever is wrong with the world primarily by teaching or making: teach people what is right or make them do what is right. The professor and policeman represent these two ways: education and law enforcement. We send people to school to teach them to live rightly and responsibly; if that doesn't work we make them do it through a system of rewards and punishments, even if it means locking them up in a jail cell.

But evil is not the greatest mystery. The mysteries of goodness and redemption exceed it, but they can be entered only when the evil is faced. These mysteries become visible in actions within the scope of simple creatures: the mournful Mundo Cani Dog's self-sacrificing death, the enigmatic Dun Cow's unscheduled visitations, Chauntecleer Rooster's canonical crows, the beautiful Pertelote Hen's forgiveness, loyal John Wesley Weasel's derring-do. These ways of being, insignificant in isolation, together and faithfully practiced, weave an intricate web that contains and restrains evil.

While I was reading this story in the seventies, I was living with a congregation that was increasingly anxious regarding the accumulation of evil rocking our country. The previous decade had seen the assassinations of President John Kennedy, his brother Robert, and the most prominent religious presence of the decade, Martin Luther King Jr. These assassinations took place against a background of fallout from the war in Vietnam, the epidemic drug culture, the sexual revolution, and the fragmentation of family, along with many doomsday radio/TV voices predicting end-times disasters and offering escape-hatch rescue operations.

I realized that Wangerin was writing his Dun Cow novels for a Christian community that was experiencing what many were diagnosing as the disintegration of a Christian culture, though not naming it as evil.

Closer to home, vocationally, I was also feeling this—feeling loneliness and isolation while working in an atmosphere dominated by leaders without humility promoting programs and strategies to save the church but coolly dismissive of a great deal of what for centuries had been the essence of church. I sensed God incarnate in Jesus being depersonalized into impersonal programs, Christ's sacrifice on the cross exchanged for consumer gratification, and the Holy Spirit mystery of worship debased into cheap entertainment.

I was not always aware of the conditions in which I was attempting to "work out my pastoral vocation (my salvation) with fear and trembling." But as the language in the church became more and more contentious, I felt more and more isolated from the work of a pastor. And I realized that the Dun Cow novels opened my spirit and imagination to the ambiguities involved in whatever is wrong with the world. There is a whole spectrum of color by which to discern goodness and truth and beauty. Black and white account for very little of it. Contention is not a fruit of the spirit.

And the mysteries involved in evil. Evil, disguised as an "angel of light," presents itself as beneficial—a good reputation, success, affluence, and—almost always—war. Too much in my culture is premised on control and know-how. That leaves far too much in soul and world untouched and unexperienced. Arrogance is not a fruit of the spirit.

The Dun Cow novels turned out to be catalytic for me in keeping the doors and windows of my imagination open to both ambiguity and mystery: the ambiguities involved in the course of everyday life in which good intentions are not always good, and the mystery of evil, hidden in the deep recesses of our awareness, unrecognizable as evil.

—∞—

All, or nearly all, of the participants in Chauntecleer's congregation, within and beyond the coop, have personal names. They are not identified according to anatomy or biology—where they occur in the orders of creation—or by their social function—the roles adopted by or assigned in the culture—but individually, by a particular name. As I read Wangerin, I was also reading the blunt statement of the great language scholar Eugen Rosenstock-Huessy that "names are the most important grammatical form in the language, any language." All other parts of speech are, or can be, lifeless, dealing objectively with what is. But names are "vehicles of spirit: they reveal social functions; they separate people and unite them."

In other words, the author intends that we, the readers, recognize the names of our friends and ourselves in these names.

And there is also this: names are seeds. When they germinate, they become stories. A seed that is not buried in the ground remains nothing but a seed. But planted it becomes, in Jesus' self-prophesy, "much fruit" (John 12:24). This was anticipated half a millennium earlier in the prophet Isaiah's vision of the "holy seed" (Isaiah 6:13) embedded in the stump of the devastated

Jerusalem temple that became the "branch" that was
Jesus Christ (Isaiah 11:1).

When the Dun Cow novel was first published (1978),
there was confusion about its genre: Children's book?
Science fiction? But now, with three Dun Cow novels in
print, there should be confusion no longer.

This is theological fiction for mature readers,
theological in the way that Faulkner and Melville,
Tolkien and Lewis are theological, grappling with
the conditions of life that force us to face the facts of
God and redemption. These stories make the obvious
luminous—that everyone counts, that everything
counts, that every creature is mysteriously beautiful,
breathtakingly important—and funny—and show that
evil breaks through the crust of our routines in an effort
to destroy the meaning, the fun, and the beauty.

C. S. Lewis held that it is only when the imagination
is kept alive by feeding it heroic legends, myths, and sagas
that it is possible to prepare the spirit to receive Christian truth in a technocratic, humanistic, and automated
age. We are in the thick of a salvation drama of cosmic
proportions, but none of the newspapers reports it and
so we overlook the obvious. In our homes, workplaces,
and churches, courageous and comic creatures surround
us. And we yawn in their faces.

And then this storyteller walks into the room and

begins to spin his story of a rooster and a coop of hens, and we wake up. Like any good storyteller, Wangerin doesn't make things up. He tells us what is happening in and around and among us but in a form and language that provokes recognition. He pulls us into an awareness of repentance, hope, and love, preparing our spirits "to receive Christian truth."

STORIES AND STORYTELLING IN SCRIPTURE AND CONGREGATION

Walt Wangerin is, more than anything else, a storyteller. He gives witness to his faith and the faith of the church primarily by telling stories to the glory of God. In this, he is in good biblical company; there is a huge precedent for the primacy given to stories in the revelation of God and of God's ways to us. In both Old and New Testament stories, the primary means of communicating God's word to us is verbal. For that we can be grateful, for story is our most accessible form of speech.

Our biblical ancestors in the faith were magnificent storytellers. The stories they told reverberate through the corridors of communities at worship and resonate in our hearts as sharply in tune with reality as when they were first told. The stories—of Adam and Eve, Abraham and Isaac, Jacob and Rachel, Moses and Joshua, Miriam and Aaron, Deborah and Barak, Ruth and Naomi, Esther and Mordecai, Joseph and Mary, Jesus and the Twelve,

Paul and Barnabas—map the country of our humanity, show its contours, reveal its dimensions. Mostly what they show is that to be human means dealing with God. And that everything we encounter and experience—birth and death, hunger and thirst, money and weapons, weather and mountains, friendship and betrayal, marriage and adultery, every nuance and detail of it—deals with God.

It is enormously significant that stories and storytelling are given such a prominent role in revealing God and God's ways to us. Young and old love stories. Literate and illiterate alike tell and listen to stories. Neither stupidity nor sophistication puts us outside the magnetic field of story. The only serious rivals to story in terms of accessibility and attraction are song and poetry, and there are plenty of those in our scriptures. When it came time for Matthew, Mark, Luke, and John to give their witness, for the most part, they have Jesus telling stories; then he became the Story.

But there is another reason for the appropriateness of story as a major means of bringing us God's word. Story doesn't just tell us something and leave it there; it invites our participation. A good storyteller gathers us into the story. We feel the emotions, get caught up in the plot, identify with the characters, see into nooks and crannies of life that we had overlooked, realize that there is more to this business of being human than we had yet explored. If the storyteller is good, doors and windows open. Our biblical storytellers were good, both in the artistic and moral senses.

One of the characteristic marks of our biblical storytellers is a certain reticence. There is an austere, spare quality to their stories. They don't tell us too much. They leave blanks in the narration, an implicit invitation to enter the story ourselves, just as we are, and find how we fit into it. These are stories that respect our freedom. They don't manipulate us; they don't force us. They show us a spacious world in which God creates and saves and blesses. First through our imaginations and then through our faith—imagination and faith are close kin here—they offer us a place in the story, invite us into this large story that takes place under the broad skies of God's purposes, in contrast to the gossipy anecdotes that we cook up in the stuffy closet of the self.

The form in which language comes to us is as important as its content. If we mistake a recipe for lamb stew for a set of clues for finding buried treasure, no matter how carefully we read it, we will end up as poor as ever and hungry besides. Ordinarily, we learn these discriminations early and give form and content equal weight in determining meaning.

But when it comes to scripture, we don't do nearly as well. Maybe it is because scripture comes to us so authoritatively—God's word—that we think all we can do is submit and obey. Submission and obedience are part of it, but first we have to listen. And listening requires listening to the way it is said (form) as well as to what is said (content).

Stories suffer misinterpretation when we don't submit to them simply as stories. We are caught off guard when divine revelation arrives in such ordinary garb and think that it's our job to dress it up in the latest Parisian silk gown of theology, or outfit it in a sturdy three-piece suit of ethics, before we can deal with it. The simple, or not so simple, story is soon, like David outfitted in Saul's armor, so encumbered with moral admonitions, theological constructs, and scholarly debates that it can hardly move. Of course there are always moral, theological, and historical elements in these stories that need to be ascertained, but never in spite of or in defiance of the story being told. One of Wangerin's tasks, which he accomplishes magnificently, is to validate the integrity of the rooster and the chickens in the coop, and at the same time give witness to the presence of God in the unlikely form of the Dun Cow, who never interferes yet is insistently, but always unobtrusively, present.

Good storytelling does not smooth over difficulties with a peppy slogan. It doesn't abstract an episode in life into a moral lesson. In a world in which God is revealed and makes covenant with us, a well-written and accurately-imagined story also reveals the difficulties and confusions we experience in such a world: the dodges and evasions of sin, the complications of family and politics, and the conditions imposed by culture, pain, and disappointment. Good storytellers keep us aware of God present and at work in what we sometimes call the secular world and our ordinary lives. But they don't do it by shouting "God!" at us. They don't bully us with moral cudgels. They tell us stories—real and realistic stories that "story" our seemingly plotless lives and open our ears and eyes to the real story, the real world, so that we can live in it with all our hearts, souls, minds, and strength.

—⁂—

It is useful to place our understanding of story in the context of Jesus. Jesus told stories. He was, as it turns out, a very good storyteller. His stories, as good stories always do, penetrate our imaginations and take on a life of their own in us. We find ourselves, often without even being aware of it, inhabiting the world of the story. Now Jesus has us where he wants us, understanding life from his point of view, seeing what reality looks like—the reality of our lives, the way we think about God and each other, from the inside, from inside the kingdom of God.

It is the devil's own work to take the stories that Jesus told (and the many others that provide so much of the content of our scriptures) and distill them down to a "truth" or a "doctrine" or a "moral" we can use without bothering with the way we use them, quite apart from people whose names we know or the local conditions in which we have responsibilities. The devil is a great intellectual; he loves getting us discussing ideas about good and evil, ideas about God, especially ideas about God. He does some of his best work when he gets us so deeply involved in ideas about God that we are hardly aware that, while we are reading or talking about God, God is actually present to us, and that the people whom he has placed in our lives to love are right there in front of us. The devil doesn't tell stories.

The stories that Jesus told were "made-up." They are what today we call fiction. Writers of fiction, the good ones, shape words and sentences in such a way that we recognize the subtle meanings and intricate connections involved in our ordinary living, meanings and connections that often go unnoticed. But the more we notice, the more we are aware and appreciate, the more we get out of life. The hidden and unnoticed elements that Jesus was particularly good at bringing to our attention are matters of God and our souls that take place in our ordinary days, in our workplace and neighborhood. After two thousand years, his parable fictions continue to wake us up to the presence and promises and demands of God implicit in the ordinary round of every ordinary day.

Fiction, with Jesus' parables serving as the parade example, is one of our most effective disciplines for spiritual formation in the Christian faith. Both writers and readers of serious fiction find themselves drawn beneath the surface appearances of their lives into the depths where God and the soul are taken seriously.

Followers of Jesus continue to tell the stories that he

told, but also go on to make up our own. After all, it is Jesus who taught us how to do it. We tell these stories to help people see the ordinary stuff and circumstances of life as already, right now, the place where God's rule is operating.

One of the welcome consequences of learning to "read" our lives in the lives of Chauntecleer and his congregation of animals is a sense of affirmation and freedom as men and women. We don't have to fit into prefabricated moral or mental or religious boxes before we are admitted into the company of God. We are taken seriously just as we are and given a place in "the land of the living" in this story that God is telling. None of us is the leading character in our own lives. The storyteller's task is not so much to present us with a moral code and tell us, "Live up to this," or set out a system of doctrine and say, "Live like this and you will live well." The storyteller says, "Live into this—this is what is involved in becoming and maturing as a child of God."

We do violence to the story if we use it for what we can get out of it or what we think will provide color and spice to our otherwise bland lives. That results in a kind of "boutique spirituality"—God as decoration, God as enhancement. In our reading, as we submit our lives to what we read, we find that we are not being led to see God in our stories, but to see ourselves in God's story.

God is the larger context and plot in which my story finds itself.

Lesslie Newbigin, in a masterful analysis and documentation of the uniqueness of the Christian faith in a pluralistic society, insists that story—not moral codes, not a list of truths—is at the very root of what we are doing and living. Nothing propositional or abstract, neither an explanation of "the way things are," nor information about eternal truths, but a story. His summarizing words: "The Christian faith, rooted in the Bible—I am convinced—primarily is to be understood as the interpretation of the story."

Singing and Preaching:
The Short Works

James Calvin Schaap

Ragman and Other Cries of Faith (1994)
Miz Lil and the Chronicles of Grace (2004)

JAMES RUSSELL LOWELL, who stood grandly among the literary luminaries of mid-nineteenth-century America, created a darling series of thumbnail sketches that featured rival poets, novelists, and essayists, many of whom have since surpassed Lowell himself in reputation. *A Fable for Critics* is Lowell's own compendium of criticism, seasoned nicely.

Interestingly, he also takes a shot at his own work and gives a self-assessment that is probably not inaccurate. "There is Lowell, who's striving Parnassus to climb," he writes. "With a whole bale of isms tied together with rhyme," a bundle his writing lugs along, he says, so heavily that "The top of the hill he will ne'er come nigh reaching." What Lowell believes about himself (but is apparently incapable of changing) is a too-dogged commitment to ideology; he knows that great writing can't attain Parnassus when it's too heavy-handed with "isms." What he needs to learn, he tells us and himself, is "the distinction 'twixt singing and preaching."

> His lyre has some chords that would ring pretty well,
> But he'd rather by half make a drum of the shell,
> And rattle away till he's old as Methusalem,
> At the head of a march to the last new Jerusalem.

James Russell Lowell thinks himself too much a preacher and not enough a singer. That he's pretty much absent from the canon suggests he may well have been right.

Traditionally, there is something about art that won't hug a pulpit. Preaching and singing are two entirely different rhetorical movements in the direction of our worship; but preaching and art move in even more distinctly different arcs. Art suggests, it entices, it begs our participation in process; preaching clarifies the straight and narrow. Art shows us a world; preaching shows us the way. Art asks us the questions that, grandly enough, have no clear answers—and takes great joy in doing just that; sermons answer those questions. Art wonders; sermons try not to. Singing—music itself—raises us to heights that some might call, and some have called, *eternal*; preaching pushes us to walk down the clear and profound and well-marked avenues of ideas. Preaching argues; art dances. Preaching is a gently prodding pointer finger; art is how we position our eyebrows.

Throughout his writing life, Walter Wangerin Jr. was, by profession, a preacher, a stemwinder in fact, the kind of minister of the gospel some folks where I live might call "a pulpiteer." Anyone who's ever heard him preach or speak knows that only a dullard or drinker could nod off in a pew or fall sleepily from a window. Pastor Walt Wangerin can hold an audience the way a maestro can an orchestra.

But he is also an artist, an accomplished novelist, poet, dramatist, and storyteller. In fact, it's fair to say of Walter Wangerin that he is both a preacher and singer because his preaching is singing; in fact, his preaching is singing even though his singing is preaching. If that feels confounding, it's because, like Lowell, we frequently find it difficult to bring the two—preaching and singing—together in any fashion whatsoever. Somehow, Walter Wangerin Jr. succeeds, and will continue to succeed, as long as God gives him breath.

Perhaps a good place from which to draw examples is the work we might call Wangerin's short fiction, stories we shouldn't really call "fiction," per se, because they are largely creative nonfiction, personal narratives with names and places and even events respectfully altered so as not to offend or besmirch—Walt is, of course, a pastor. *Miz Lil and the Chronicles of Grace* includes a dozen such hybrid tales, part fiction and part sermon all at once. These "chronicles" are imbued with enough fiction to keep them from being history, enough history to keep them from being fiction, *and*, amazingly, they preach. "The stories told in this book are true," Wangerin says in an introduction. "They happened." But then he goes on to say that what he's put on paper is not exactly what happened, even though what actually happened is something very much akin to the stories he is going to tell. "I've made an aesthetic and ethical decision sometimes to conflate events, sometimes to create a single fictional character from a composite of many people, and sometimes to invent the detail and the character which the deeper spirit of the story required." This prelude in his preface is a blessed admission because it frees readers, after a fashion, from using verisimilitude or the idea of the "felt truth" of a story in any kind of strict fashion to evaluate or critique the stories themselves. It's also plainly honest for him to say what he does, especially in a day in which too many memoirists have crafted their stories and thus tarnished the reputation of a genre that promises only "the whole truth." Wangerin's stories in *Miz Lil*, these "chronicles of grace," as he calls them, aren't meant to be true to reality, per se; neither are they intended to be, literally, literary descendants of the stories of Sherwood Anderson, say, or William Faulkner or Alice Munro, each of whom found the world on their own square inch of human turf. They're not fiction really, either.

Still, Wangerin is enough of an artist to know that his work will fail if it is not true to "reality." What Wangerin intends that his stories be is, first and foremost, *eternally* true. Thus, Wangerin doesn't necessarily hang his clerical robe in the closet to do his storytelling. He wants to be both an artist and a preacher.

He's transparent about that relationship in the essay "Preaching" from *Ragman and Other Cries of Faith*, where he explains his vision of preaching through an essay that clearly addresses other preachers. What he advises them to do, in no uncertain terms, is to tell stories. He can't say it emphatically enough, it seems. "Story is word and experience communicated," he tells them. Then, "—tell stories. It is the fullness of witness."

Clearly, Rev. Walter Wangerin Jr. believes that the very best sermons *are* stories.

And that's why *Miz Lil and the Chronicles of Grace*, as well as that seeming follow-up collection, *Ragman and Other Cries of Faith*, are what we might call "Christian" literature, a description that has its own myriad problems, but a classification that is germane in surveying both Wangerin's methodology and his work. There's little doubt that in *Miz Lil* and *Ragman* his most attentive audience will be believers; they're the readers who understand most about the substance of the stories he tells. Having said that, however, I believe the stories' major themes often only tangentially "preach" Christian doctrine or moral convictions. At their best, they are "of this world" yet offer and suggest the reality of the eternal. But the landscape on which they happen is a turf that's not at all unfamiliar to Christian believers.

SPITTIN' IMAGE

"The Spittin' Image" is a story/essay/memoir, a "chronicle of grace," an artful sermon, even though the centerpiece is simply Wangerin's own misreading of an assessment given by one of his parishioners a quarter century after Wangerin's mother told him he was "the spittin' image" of his grandfather. Musette Bias, a woman with a broad Southern drawl, describes her son with the same phrase. When Wangerin can't believe she'd used the same expression, he asks Ms. Bias for clarification and gets it forthwith. His ears had somehow garbled what she'd said. What Ms. Bias meant was "spirit an' image" of her son's father. It's Wangerin's mishearing of the phrase that triggers the entire story.

Even though Walt himself is both a central and dynamic character, as he is most often in this collection, his grandfather's colorful character is the narrative's major attraction. We meet Grandpa Storck via a description that is as concrete and convincing as any in the collection. "Grandpa seldom smiled. He had an eruption of moustache beneath his nose, like white smoke from the chimney pots of his nostrils. His face was mostly expressive of one mood only: solemnity, rectitude, Lutheran doom.

His arms were long and strong, his hands huge, his stride unhalting, his whole body an uncompromising dogma. Moses! Grandpa Storck, his hair like cloud at the top of his head, was an immediate Sinai, grim and untender— but I was not intimidated." The story has other and greater concerns than Grandpa Storck, but Wangerin pays loving homage to his sanctified grandfather, whose face is festooned with "eruption of moustache." One telling anecdote happens out back of the barn, in a spot Wangerin says the old man (a man whose very presence was "uncompromising dogma") considered his own special and secret place. Together they share a very human moment. "And thus it was that sometime that summer we stood side by side, my grandpa and myself, solemnly facing the same wall in a wordless fellowship, bowing our heads as devoutly as though we prayed, but peeing. This was a holy moment, and I knew it. For we were man and boy together, little and large, absolutely intimates, members of a proud society, and in love." The sermon Wangerin is preaching here, not without a smirk, incorporates both earth and sky delightfully.

Grandpa Storck chewed tobacco, which prompts Wangerin to spin one of the most encyclopedic meditations on "spittin'" in American literature. His regard for his grandfather is immense, and he is spellbound by the man who tells him stories about the cemetery he maintained, tales of the dying, and of what happens to bodies in the grave. Little Wally gets lost in the telling.

More than anything else, what Walt Wangerin remembers of his grandfather, however, is love—the love he's sure Grandpa Storck had for him, a love he notes for the last time when Grandpa Storck is dying, a time when, once again, Wally Wangerin sees his grandfather's grand smile. "For everything else can change in mortality, everything except this one thing: the smile that love engenders. And then nothing else is important anymore. Grandpa smiled and suddenly this was my Grandpa Storck. And he smiled at me, so I was there as well. In a flood I felt a freedom, I felt me come to be."

Had the essay/story/memoir ended here—and it might have in the hands of a lesser writer—it would have been touching, although maybe a tad self-centered. But there was more. Two weeks later, when the phone call notifying his mother of Grandpa's death finally comes, young Walt doesn't know what to say to her so he offers her his hand to shake, just as he had offered his grandpa a handshake on his deathbed; and the odd little gesture is accepted adoringly with hugs and kisses—*and* with the description that began the story: "You are the spittin' image of your grandpa."

Once more, in the hands of a lesser writer, the story could have ended there; but Wangerin has more on his mind than a family narrative. "Some twenty-seven years thereafter," he says, and in a single line we move into another moment of sorrow, where we meet "a strong-boned, strong-hearted woman as capable of love as any of my forebears, but nowhere near as stern in Lutheran rectitude. Lutheran she was. German she was not. Her love had no hard edges." That woman, Musette Bias, repeats the phrase in a fashion that brings both his mother's words and his grandfather's life to mind immediately.

"Did you say 'spit'?" he asks her.

Musette Bias says no. "I said spee-it." And that explanation moves everything he's told us earlier in the story to another level of intent and meaning.

The power of the story doesn't lie solely in some delightful lingual nuance. "Spittin' Image" is a memorable story because of Grandpa Storck's humanness amid his only occasional smiles; because of Walt's mother's difficulty in expressing love herself—even to her son; because of Wally's own growing understanding of family and love; and because of a sudden glorious expansion of plain old cliché into spiritual epiphany, a moment Wangerin himself would never forget: "I did more than look like Grandpa Storck. His spirit, the character and the force of his being, dwelt within me," he says.

Ms. Bias's explanation of the words she used creates the bridge by which a boy who'd become a preacher a quarter century later comes to understand himself and the qualities he was granted by his own grandfather.

Yet one more little plot twist offers delightful end punctuation. One of Grandpa Storck's cemetery stories explained how it was that bodies changed after death.

"*Junge! Did you know that a dead man, he don't die all at once?*" he'd asked his grandson years earlier, then told the boy, memorably, about long hair and curled fingernails.

In the last paragraph or two of the story Wangerin returns to that question and description, but with new and radiant illumination of spirit. "And the boy, before he followed time from grace, said, *Yes, old man, I know.*"

So what is this story, one of many such in the collection? Is it a story? An essay? A memoir? A sermon?

All of the above. What grants the story its grace is concrete descriptions that jump off the page, anecdotes that fill out character by showing and not telling, and an unfolding plot line that offers continuing surprises, including a conclusion gently shaped from the range of our own expectations, a conclusion which serves to satisfy us, as stories do, even more. The best endings, good writers say, are the ones that are totally unexpected and yet perfectly predictable, and thus, artistically rendered.

Is a little narrative like this "Christian" writing? After all, it's only tangentially about "spirit," and "spirit" itself is very much lowercase. If a reader wants to affix an uppercase S, he or she can—and the story works, sort of, but not well. What's more, the essence of the story—even though it exists in a broader setting in which Christ the King is never really absent and always respected—is no more or less than perfectly human, our narrator learning only how it is that he and his grandfather, his loving grandfather, are "spiritually" related.

Most of the stories in *Miz Lil* operate in the very same fashion—story as sermon, sermon as story.

An old novelist friend of mine used to say that all stories are circular, after a fashion. The ones shaped like *O*s are complete and, well, finished. The reader has little difficulty appreciating them because they finish by completing, fully, what they began. The ones that are *C*s, he said, are often stronger and require more actively participating readers because those stories leave a gap, fully expecting that we'll fill in what they don't tell us. The best stories make us a part of them. Then again, some stories are almost *I*s, in that discovering their circular character makes demands many readers are not interested in fulfilling.

What about "The Spittin' Image"? No questions remain afterwards. The narrative completes itself, leaves nothing unraveled or incomplete. In that sense, the story is an *O*, a kind of sermon. It answers the questions it raises. Still, the path to discovery is bright and wily, and the plot line moves in unexpected ways. So while the story may well complete itself, in achievement, it's not without its joys and delights.

What Wangerin insists on in his stories, however, is what he calls "edification." In an essay in *Ragman*, titled "Edification/Demolition," he offers that there are basically only two ways of greeting others in this world and two ways of leaving them. He's not simply talking about readers here, but people walking down everyday sidewalks. Still, the injunction the preacher gives the congregation extends even to the preacher's storytelling:

> Every time you meet another human being, you have the opportunity. It's a chance at holiness. For you will do one of two things, then. Either you will build him up, or you will tear him down. Either you will acknowledge that he is, or you will make him sorry that he is—sorry, at least, that he is there, in front of you. You will create, or you will destroy. And the things you dignify or deny are God's own property. They are made, each of them, in his own image.

Anyone familiar with the literary work of Walter Wangerin Jr. will testify, I think, to the fact that this basic definition of human behavior is a truth that dominates his own storytelling as well. He believes the stories he tells will either create or destroy, edify or demolish, and that our responsibility as believers in God, as writers or as nonwriters, is created specifically by a faith that stoutly maintains that all of those we meet, regardless of circumstance or color or station in life, are made, "each of them, in his own image."

FIVE COVENANTS OF A CHRISTIAN WRITER

This basic tenet of Wangerin's writing is clearly testified to in a handout he gave his students, a handout meant to provide young writers with an initial understanding of their task as believers commissioned by character and calling to write stories, to write as Wangerin himself has. My copy of those precepts, "The Five Covenants of a Christian Writer," is a series of pledges that are themselves instructive in understanding the questions posed by so much of Wangerin's work, and so visible in his short narratives. They spell out what Prof. Walter Wangerin wanted to see in his student writers, but also what he expected of himself.

The first covenant or promise pertains to seeing clearly, to "General Reality":

> GENERAL REALITY. I promise to be true to what I see around me, to what I know by my own faculties—my sense perceptions, my experience, my sense of truth—to be the world as we all know it.

If it weren't for the final clause, evaluating Wangerin's own writing—or anyone else's, for that matter—would be impossible, should we desire to do so. But that final phrase, "as we all know it," encourages us to use our own experience in evaluation: when a character's actions, for example, seem far from what we know of human behavior, we wince or raise an eyebrow and the fictional dream, as John Gardner would say, dissolves immediately. Writers can and do commit falsehood in the name of higher truth; they fabricate human character in order to accomplish preexisting goals in their writing.

Tired of the lambasting Barbara Kingsolver gives missionaries in *The Poisonwood Bible*? Write your own mission novel and redeem "the missionary" from the deformities so endemic in that novel. But if your aim is at something other than what it means, as you know it, to be human, you're not being true to what you know by sense, by experience, by truth itself, Wangerin might say. He wants his students to pledge fidelity to what they know and see around them; he expects such fidelity from himself as well.

Only once in my multiple readings of Wangerin's short tales did I stop and question verisimilitude, and that was in the story "Robert" in *Miz Lil*, one of several stories in that collection to document Wangerin's own initiation into the rigors of the ministry in the inner city, where he had to learn to be himself. Robert, homeless and a bother with his ridiculous umbrella/cane, comes marching up to the front of the church one Sunday morning, listening to the beat of his own drum, as if mad or drunk, full of a desire to pray. Sadly, Wangerin's commitment to form and ritual can't abide such unscheduled behavior. He was just then ending his sermon, undoubtedly with a flourish.

Readers have no difficulty accepting the reality of the situation, but some, like me, might have problems believing Wangerin's own behavior at that moment, though he, as the author, works hard at building motivation for his own anger. He says he stared at Robert in an effort to get him to stop from praying, but "an angelic expression flooded his features, a radiance as though he were overwhelmed by the pure, supernal beauty of his promise."

If "less is more," as Mies van der Rohe once canonized, then we seemed aimed in an opposite direction. One gets a clear sense of where the story is moving. But what's somehow unnecessary and even overdrawn is the tumult of the preacher's anger. "Panic gave me a tongue," he writes, and he yells (upper case) at Robert not to pray.

The homeless man is undeterred and announces before the entire congregation once again that he has committed his heart, mind, and soul to call upon the name of the Lord.

"I leaped at the man," Wangerin remembers. "I flew at him and grabbed his shoulders, one in either hand. 'Robert,' I cried directly into his face with desperate authority, 'you *can't* pray.'"

This reader feels manipulated at this moment, even though it may well be manipulation for the best of reasons: Wangerin wants us in the position he found himself, somehow believing he could and should deny Robert access to God because the man wasn't doing worship right. This story is headed for a noble end—a lesson in humility; but my skepticism argues that there's fabrication to reach those ends. Wangerin gets there by faulty means, or so says my critical soul.

Whether or not what actually happened that moment in Grace Church was what he says it was in the story is of little matter in judging the veracity of the narration. The moment feels overplayed. Wangerin seems more interested in idea than he does in human character, more anxious, in other words, to preach than to sing.

He does well to remind his students of their own obligations to their "sense of truth—to be the world as we all know it." He knows himself that it's an easy promise to break, especially, perhaps, for Christian writers.

> KNOWLEDGE OF CRAFT. I promise to know all I can about the art of fiction, to read its practitioners, to understand what gifted writers describe as its nature and function.

Oddly enough, many more people in our culture want to write a book than read one. Perhaps one shouldn't consider that fact odd, because all of us have a story and most of us, given the right prompt, will share it, save a chapter or two held back out of propriety or embarrassment. If you want to play rugby, Wangerin is saying, watch how rugby is played by the finest in the world, and promise yourself that you'll always be a student of the game.

In an essay he wrote for *More Than Words*, a volume of essays by Christian writers who describe the influence of a particular writer on them and their work, Walter Wangerin talked about the significance of a thousand

and one nights, bedside, with the tales of Hans Christian Andersen.

> Andersen's fantasies schooled me . . . in realism. I know no resurrection except that first there's been a death. And as a writer, I cannot speak genuinely or deeply of resurrection except I speak the same of death and the sin that engendered death. That I can speak accurately of death without despairing is hardly melancholic. It is liberty—and victory ("O Death, where is thy sting?"). It is the evidence of the fundamental influence which Hans Christian Andersen had upon a child who did not analyze but lived such stories as Little Claus and Big Claus.

What Wangerin learned from the bedtimes during which his father read Andersen's tales to him was the importance of a reader *experiencing* the story, not merely reading it. That characteristic and quality is, without a doubt, present in everything he has ever written. It's clear that Wangerin wants more than anything to capture the reader in the way that Hans Christian Andersen did.

> AUDIENCE. I promise never to cheat on my readers, to do the best I can not to deliberately deceive or manipulate.

When Wangerin encourages his students not to manipulate their audience, it is a reminder to avoid a strategy that altogether too many Christian writers not

only employ but, as they set the pen to the paper or their
fingers to the keys, actually set out to do. When there
is a greater goal than the truth itself, when the goal is
the beauty of some *ism*, as James Russell Lowell said,
characters and action get flattened in order to convey or
even sell an ideology or a faith. Writing weakens when
it's about idea and not character. Christian writers, like
other writers who lug *isms* into their work, may well
manipulate and excuse themselves for it because, after
all, it's eternity with Jesus they're selling. But, as Lowell
knew, they put the integrity of their work at risk. They'll
be preaching, not singing.

The third covenant asks beginning writers to avoid
deceiving or manipulating for any reason whatsoever, to
remain true to what Wangerin himself would describe
as, I'm sure, the high calling of the writer.

One can be confident that each of these promises
is generated from real-life experience. In "Robert," for
instance, Wangerin sadly admits to a propensity in his
own rhetoric that he, in his passion to communicate the
gospel truth, occasionally exercises. "Now I will admit
that when I'm straining I tend to raise my voice," he
writes of his preaching style, "that sometimes I overcompensate with a forced dramatic vigor. This could be
dangerous, if someone is inclined to react more to the
noise than to the instruction."

What he obviously has discovered is that it's entirely
possible for well-meaning writers to "overcompensate

with a forced dramatic vigor," to manipulate, in other words, a penchant that is simply a lighter grade of deception, but deception, nevertheless.

> COMMUNITY. I promise never to use my family, my friends, my close acquaintances, my circles, my community, in any way which will hurt them or alter their lives for my gain or the purposes of my work.

What Wangerin asks his students to consider here is a commitment most writers would find impossible—a promise not to say things about people they know in a fashion that will in any way injure them.

Writers always pick and choose from the life experiences that accumulate in the heart and soul. I once asked Eugene Peterson how much of him is in the translation work he did in order to create *The Message*. He told me that he is in every word. I mention that only because it's virtually impossible not to assume that the stories or poems or essays a writer produces are entirely drawn from the imagination. I have no doubt, for instance, that Wangerin himself would admit that Chauntecleer the Rooster, from *The Book of the Dun Cow*, is imbued with characteristics drawn from very real people who lived and moved and had their being in Wangerin's own life. He may not want to admit who those prototypes are or were, and he may have successfully camouflaged the prototypes so that no one really knows for sure, but creating stories without drawing, in one way or another, on the album of characters one has met or known throughout life is difficult.

Still, using real people, even as prototypes, raises moral questions for those who do not want to hurt those close to them. In my own life as a writer, for instance, my father disliked two of the novels I wrote. In one, he was confident that readers would read him into the iron-fisted, guilt-ridden father. Nothing could have been further from the truth. No matter—my father was hurt by the novel. Another strong figure in a second novel was far closer to the father I knew as a boy; that novel also distressed him because the weaknesses in the character he understood as his own.

When my daughter was twelve years old, she came into my study holding a book of devotionals I'd written and published, devotions for kids, in fact, and told me in no uncertain terms that I was not to write another word about her in any book whatsoever until she had read the passage and given me permission.

None of these "covenants" are easy to fulfill, maybe especially not this one because of the near impossibility of never relying in some way on prototypes in the work writers create. A strict reading of this particular promise might well have kept me from writing and publishing either novel or the meditations, because of the possibility of hurting members of my family.

The difficulties a pastor encounters in writing fiction are even greater, given that a pastor deals in real stories more often than almost anyone who is not in a similar position of moral and spiritual leadership. Preachers, like doctors and lawyers, are given expressly different directives in court proceedings because what is said in the study is inviolably private. When a pastor positions his or her fingers over the keys to draft a story, the likelihood that the line that emerges on the page will carry some inkling of stories told by his parishioners in that very study is far greater than it would be in a study of any other writer who doesn't regularly hear confessions. For a preacher to tell those stories directly is not only egregious but also punishable by law.

It would be interesting to know what literal truth there is in Wangerin's description of Arthur Forte in *Ragman*, because what Wangerin says of him is not becoming.

> After several months of chair-sitting, both Arthur and his room were filthy. I do not exaggerate: roaches flowed from my step like puddles stomped in; they dropped causally from the walls. I stood very still. The TV flickered constantly. There were newspapers strewn all over the floor. There lay a damp film on every solid object in the room, from which arose a close, moldy odor, as though it were alive and sweating. But the dampness was a blessing, because Arthur smoked.

This story is yet another narrative in which a young preacher comes to learn something about the realities of life lived by the people he is given to love and serve. It's a

beautiful story, made so, I would suggest, by the squalor
in which it is set. If Arthur Forte were a rich man or if he
was even ordinary, there would be no story. The story's
strength is created by the fact that we too have to look
away.

Was there an Arthur Forte? Did a man the young
preacher knew live in that kind of roach-infested apart-
ment? And if there was such a man, might he have been
hurt by reading about himself or his surroundings in a
story his own pastor wrote?

Wangerin himself answers these questions in a
fashion that may not satisfy his readers: "Like Cyrus to
the Jews," he says, "Arthur Forte is anointed of God to
set me free." Forte's story is Wangerin's own testimony.

Whether or not the stories in *Miz Lil* or *Ragman*
ever reached back into the psyches of those Wangerin
might have used as prototypes is a question that cannot
be answered here. Whether Miz Lil or Ragman or Arthur
Forte, or whomever they might have been patterned after
from real life, ever felt offended by being part of a story,
or a fiction, we'll never know. But the moral question
is profound and completely understandable when one
describes the phenomenon we are talking about in
this usage: *writers use people they know.* What is never
particularly saintly is *using* people, not even when the
end in question might be.

Once again, what I am trying to establish is that the
covenants Walter Wangerin gave his writing students

through the years involve principles that set out the general dimensions for doing imaginative work as believers, principles that ask students to commit to standards that are exacting, standards shared only by other writers with a similar significant commitment to their work, a commitment to be a part of Christ's own kingdom.

When any writer determines not to "use my family, my friends, my close acquaintances, my circles, my community, in any way which will hurt them," that determination has a price, and is undertaken only because some things in life, for the writer, are more important than writing. That simple truth may well describe the contours of Christian writing better than any other attempt at definition: a Christian writer is someone whose commitments go beyond the work.

The final covenant is more existential, but no less exacting:

> WORLDVIEW. I promise not to violate those attitudes that comprise my most important beliefs about God and his relationship to the world he has created.

Walter Wangerin is asking his students to be both student and teacher in the writing process, to do something only they are capable of doing: to determine whether their imaginative work honors their own "important beliefs about God and his relationship to the world."

Again, what the directive asks isn't easy. Most writers like to think about writing itself as an exercise in discovery, a means of determining truth that is almost as revelatory as, say, the scientific method. "I write because I don't know what I think until I read what I say," or so said Flannery O'Connor, one of the most celebrated Christian writers of the twentieth century. If O'Connor is right—if writing is an act of discovery, and many believe it is—then the promise which Wangerin wishes to exact from his students could well close off the blessed inquiry O'Connor appreciated and that imagination almost certainly evokes.

It would be difficult for me to believe that Walter Wangerin Jr. disagrees with Flannery O'Connor here. Were we to ask him whether he had learned things by way of his exploration of the life of the apostle Paul in *Paul: A Novel*, or of the life of Christ in *Jesus: A Novel*, it's difficult for anyone to imagine that he would say he did not. Life is learning.

So how, finally, does Walter Wangerin Jr. negotiate the difficult terrain which normally separates singing and preaching?

He creates a bridge between singing and preaching by making himself the curriculum, by making himself the material for his stories, making himself the story. "I risk the disclosure of myself and my experience," he says in "Preaching." And then, "I present you with the very stuff itself of the events that have shaped this person before you, and so reveal the Shaper shaping. By these stories I am sinfully, gracefully whole, and whole may be the drama of God in me."

But there's more. He warns preachers about the vapid doctrine that doesn't begin to show what we can see of God's imminence, about thinking of that characteristic of the Maker of Heaven and Earth as a plank in some creaking theological infrastructure. "So long as it remains a doctrine alone, a truth to be taught, immanence itself continues an abstraction—and is not imminent," he says.

The answer to that problem is simple, says the preacher: "God appears imminent in human events. I am more than a preacher. I am myself the preaching. For God chooses to touch me whole, not only in my mind." Thus, the experiences he recounts, shaped and reshaped by his own promises, his covenants, become the art, as he is, himself, he says, the sermon.

There's a kind of bravado to all of this that is almost Emersonian, in a way—writer as both chronicler and character, as artist and pallete, as singer and song. All of which may be the means by which to understand just exactly how it is Walt Wangerin has been doing, throughout his life, what seems otherwise nearly impossible—to be both preacher and singer.

"Make of yourselves a parable," he says to the preachers in that essay, "—tell stories. It is the fullness of witness."

I heard Walt hold forth before I ever read him. It was the early '80s, at a writing conference at Concordia in Wisconsin, which happens to have been one of his own alma maters back when he was a boy and it was a preparatory seminary. Wangerin was—and remains—a presence, and his plenary session, as I remember, walked a line between deep appreciation for his Concordia past and steep antipathy for the difficulties many kids face when thrown too innocently into boarding school life.

But when sometime later I read *Miz Lil and the Chronicles of Grace*, I shivered, so sure I was that what I was reading was what I wanted to create, what I wanted to be—a writer, an artist, who was, in fact, a preacher, someone who could craft whole worlds and not renege in the least on the bounty of grace that empowers that vision. I remember putting that collection of tales up in my study library in a place where it would not be lost—it was that important.

There was perhaps more to my deep regard for *Miz Lil* than craft; there was also Wangerin's continuing use of a coming-of-age motif in that collection of chronicles. Just about every narrative features him learning something important, whether as a kid on the way to school or a young preacher on the tough streets of an inner city, it took him more than a few scrapes to understand.

Even though I was well into my thirties, I was myself coming of age—new father, new writer, new college prof.

Coming-of-age stories are bountiful because we all

have them stored away in our closets, moments when suddenly the world becomes something other than it has always been. Some writers I know claim that each of us has only one story to tell, really—the story of the time we learned something that catapulted us into adulthood, from innocence to experience.

In the '80s, I was feeling my way blindly into dreams of what I might become as a writer, a Christian writer, and Wangerin's *Miz Lil* was by far the most memorable text in my writing education. Here was someone who could do it all, who could write absolutely captivating paragraphs about spittin' tobacco without shying away from the love and grace that illuminated his vision and his world.

Walter Wangerin believes the stories he tells, the stories we all tell, create or destroy, edify or demolish, and that our responsibility as believers is created from the conviction that those we meet, all of them, regardless of circumstance or color or station in life, are made, "each of them, in his own image." For years, in my classes, I also have told students that to me, being a Christian and a writer means being a prophet of hope, a variation on a Wangerin theme.

Way back when, Walt Wangerin modeled for me what it meant to be both a believer and a writer. Soon, now, *Miz Lil* will go back in the stacks, finding its place on a brand-new shelf of books in my own brand-new study.

But I'll always know where it stands.

The Sun with Bites Taken Out

Diane Glancy

"And he shall be as the light of the morning, when the
sun riseth, even a morning without clouds"
—2 Samuel 23:4

The Crying for a Vision (1994)

Summary: Waskn Mani, "Moves Walking," the son
of a Lakota woman and a star in the sky, is caught
between the spiritual world of his elders and a one-
eyed warrior Fire Thunder who first comes bearing
buffalo meat, but soon becomes a threat.

I WILL TALK ABOUT *The Crying for a Vision*, but I
want to speak my way into the book first.

I began teaching Native American Literature
twenty-five years ago. The theme of most of the books
I taught was re-creating meaning from loss. In many
of the books, the re-creation process began by telling
a story, making a structure of words from which came

understanding and renewal even after the story was told. Our language, after all, is our most fundamental tool. Words are living beings. They have a presence just as the land, the elements, the animals, the people do.

The native culture is based on oral tradition. At the center of its structure is an energy field, a spider spinning a web that radiates outward from the core, catching the rays of the sun, implicating the enormity of the solar system in a few small strands. Somehow it seems to me the way God works. We are the smallness of his creation in proportion to the universe, yet we carry his enormity within us, or part of it, or a similitude of it. It's beyond what I can understand or explain—this pattern of the large within the small. This pattern in the small that carries an implication of the large. It also is the way literature works, or should work.

⁂

The most significant piece of native literature, in my opinion, is *Black Elk Speaks*. It holds the magic of the process of storytelling. It contains, at the heart, the message of Christ. Ironically, it is written by a white man, John G. Neihardt, who visited Black Elk in Mandan, South Dakota, in 1930–32. Neihardt's daughter, Enid, took down Black Elk's words, which had been translated by his cousins from Lakota into English. Later, Neihardt transcribed Enid's notes, some of which were in shorthand. How could all this make sense? I thought of the books of the Bible written by different people over many years in different places. Yet somehow, both narratives hold together.

"Because no good thing can be done by any man alone, I will first make an offering and send a voice to the Spirit of the World, that it may help me to be true." Black Elk begins his story just a few years before the coming of the Wasichus, the white man. Black Elk speaks of hunting bison, of different ceremonies of the Lakota people, of various skirmishes with other tribes and eventually the U.S. soldiers, many of them led by George Custer. Black Elk also talked about the Wounded Knee Massacre and the Ghost Dance that preceded it. He shares his visions and what he felt were his failures as he witnessed the end of the Plains Indian's way of life. "I know it was the story of a mighty vision given to a man too weak to use it; of a holy tree that should have flourished in a people's heart with flowers and singing birds, and now it is withered; and of a people's dream that died in the bloody snow." That bloody snow was the Massacre at Wounded Knee, December 29, 1890, when the 7th Cavalry murdered the last of the Ghost Dancers. Vine Deloria Jr. remarked that "the book has become a North American bible of all tribes."

In the chapter "The Messiah," Christ visits the Indians who were seeking a way out of extinction during the Ghost Dance. He also was called Wanekia, "The

One Who Makes Live," and Wovoka, and Jack Wilson. Was this Christ showing himself to the Indians? Was it a ploy? Who knows what really happened. The truth of the matter is in its various possibilities. It is another mystery. "The sacred man gave some sacred red paint and two eagle feathers to Good Thunder. The people must put this paint on their faces and they must dance a ghost dance that the sacred man taught to Good Thunder, Yellow Breast, and Brave Bear. If they did this, they could get on this other world when it came."

I actually took Epic America, a class taught by John Neihardt at the University of Missouri. It must have been 1960. It was in one of those large lecture halls that held 500 students. The rows of seats descended to a stage where Neihardt sat in a chair. I was on the back row, of course. All I could see was his mop of white hair. He looked like a small star in the distance. A spark of white. It was a dark time. School was difficult. But there was John Neihardt talking about the land and the Indians, and I was there as one of the invisible ones. But I was taking a bite of that bright light, education. It would be worth it someday.

⁂

The first time I read Wangerin's *The Crying for a Vision*, I saw the energy and vision of *Black Elk Speaks*. Wangerin's book is the weaving of a web. It echoes that spark of creation when God spoke the world into being. As a Christian, I see Jesus as the Word telling God's story. I saw that same message in *Black Elk Speaks*.

I consider *Black Elk Speaks* the foundation of native literature. In addition, I taught four other novels as the four cornerstones. Native American Literature is usually a depressing literature about alcoholism and disenfranchisement. "I am as distant from myself as the moon," James Welch writes in *Winter in the Blood*. Students often were disappointed. They thought we would study nature. Spirituality. That we would commune with something other than loss and anger.

In Scott Momaday's *House Made of Dawn*, Abel suffers post-traumatic stress disorder after WWII. He wanders around Los Angeles and finally returns to his reservation in New Mexico to run a race and greet the dawn, accompanied by a sacred song. That ceremony is the book's answer to re-establishing meaning. In Leslie Silko's *Ceremony*, Tayo goes to a traditional medicine man who does not help his PTSD. He finally visits a new style medicine man on a hill above Gallup. "Tell me your story," the man says. Responsibility and guarding against evil is part of it too. In the third cornerstone, *Winter in the Blood*, there is no ceremony. The nameless narrator wanders Highway 2 in Montana looking for his razor and gun that a girlfriend stole. There is no ceremony. No meaning. It is the story of having no story. Get used to nothing. The fourth cornerstone is *Love Medicine*, in which Louise Erdrich tells stories of the faulty little medicine bag of the human heart capable of love and forgiveness.

Each semester I added new books to keep myself interested, but these four remained. Five books, actually, including *Black Elk Speaks*. But it stood apart from the others. It was a holy book. All of them told a story in their own way. I know of courses on Native American Literature where these books are not listed. For me, they are central. I did not see how I could teach NA Lit without them. They were part of my own searching also. How to walk in a mixed-blood tradition. Not only between native and European parents, but also within a syncretism of Christian faith and tradition.

LIGHT WITH PART OF IT MISSING: FINDING A CONNECTION

How could I remain a Christian in a secular college that did not honor faith? How could I believe in Christ whom many natives were against because churches organized most boarding schools and students were punished for using their native language? The boarding schools were punitive. They tried to remove the culture—the heartbeat of native heritage. I have sat on panels before and heard the anger still in the throats of those who had boarding school experiences or whose parents had suffered boarding school education.

On one hand, education is light. On the other hand, to receive an American education, for the native, is to be given the light with part of it missing—namely, the native way of seeing the world. To them, a European education is only a portion of the light, and a small one at that. A small portion with teeth. The education process for the native is hurtful. It is light and it is also death, with all the inherent complications, dichotomies, and oppositions.

At the University of Missouri, from time to time, I sat in a small church near campus. I don't remember praying or asking anything. Maybe I was silently absorbing faith and the strength it provides.

⊸⊷

Many of the students I later had in my Native American Literature classes seemed to feel privileged. They didn't need to know the sludge. They had been given medals and trophies for every sport since childhood. They had received honors, and they would continue to receive honors. They would receive by their very act of being there. What is it with the alcoholism? The depressing stories? The woman with eight children by as many men, with crocheted doilies on the arms and backs of the chairs in her tidy trailer? What relevance is that to our privileged lives? What's up with these books? The Indians lived in America for thousands of years and never made any progress. We are the ones who came and made it the nation it is.

Native American Literature provides a missing part in the curriculum of the history and understanding of America, in my opinion. Its stories and literature are a part of the story of the continent. The land holds stories of those who lived upon it, even if seen as the minor ones.

In the first reading of *The Crying for a Vision*, I was struck with the similarity to *Black Elk Speaks*. They were very different books, yet Wangerin's novel followed in the vein of *Black Elk Speaks*. *The Crying for a Vision* was a fictional story. *Black Elk Speaks* was nonfiction. But the struggle was the same. There is even someone named Black Elk in *The Crying for a Vision*. I wasn't sure if it was *the* Black Elk or a character with the same name.

The second time was a different story. I had taught Native American Literature for years. I had retired. Put it away. I had trouble getting back into the book. I didn't want to go. Maybe I felt like the students I'd had many years earlier. Maybe I had moved onto other things. My interests had taken a Christian turn. But what did Wangerin's book contain, if not an underlying Christian message?

Matthew Dickerson, when he asked me to write this chapter, helped me by providing a connection to my own story. He pointed out that *The Crying for a Vision* is set among the Lakota people of the northern plains of America in the time before the coming of Europeans and their Christian religion. The story's protagonist wrestles with the tension between the calling of God and some of the competing traditions and ways of his people. Although my own ancestry is half Cherokee and not Lakota, I grew up with a similar tension between a Christian faith I claimed as my own and my native ancestry, with its traditions and myths, which I also claimed and continue to claim. Could I hold to both of these? How? What happens when the traditions seem to conflict?

What Wangerin's story does, Dickerson adds, is find a way through the tension, without either ignoring it, or reducing it to formulas and platitudes, or minimizing the personal cost of following that path. Wangerin offers this path by seeing within the very stories and traditions and myths of the Lakota people—stories he learned by spending time among them—a deeper truth that points to the Gospel even if the stories never mention Jesus by his Hebrew or European names. This is also what Paul does in his sermon in Athens (Acts 17), showing that their very own myths and stories of the unknown God, and the words of their prophets and poets, point the way toward Christ. Later writers such as J. R. R. Tolkien and C. S. Lewis drew from pagan Norse and Germanic myths to point the way toward the true God. So Wangerin does with the myths, stories, and traditions of the people of this tale.

I also have felt the tensions between The Maker or God or the Great Spirit and native traditions, which often seem to be going their own way. How to breach both. How to hold a different culture and the message of Christ. I once said it was like having one foot on the dock and the other on an unmoored rowboat. *The Crying for a Vision* and *Black Elk Speaks* helped to bridge that gap.

I was also rereading 2 Samuel the second time I picked up the book. The villain, Fire Thunder, was something like Joab, the general of David's army and a warrior who thought nothing of murdering anyone in his way. He killed Amasa, Abner, and Absalom, and finally dies by the sword himself in 1 Kings 2:34 because David, on his deathbed, asked Solomon for Joab's life.

As I read *The Crying for a Vision*, I kept seeing it in terms of its biblical references, or what seemed to be its biblical references. Maybe the novel is an allegory. Or a type of allegory. Moves Walking, the hero, is a type of David, a man of war, a man of passion and song. Or maybe Moves Walking is more of a Christ figure with the good of his tribe at heart. The novel certainly is about good and evil, light and dark.

As the story begins, Moves Walking is a five-year-old Lakota boy. He is in the tipi with his grandmother and an elder, Slow Buffalo. Moves Walking is an orphan, or so it seems, until the hunter/villain, Fire Thunder, arrives with buffalo meat, driving the herd toward the tribe so they can have more meat. "Father," Moves Walking says to him. But when Moves Walking mentions his mother's name, Rattling Hail Woman, Fire Thunder

> rose from the ground with so horrible a roar that the drumbeat froze on the air and the dancing stopped and the whole village turned to see what happened. This is what they saw: they saw the warrior standing at full height above the boy who bent down in a crouch as if praying. In the warrior's right hand was a knife raised on high. . . . The boy was not praying. He was bleeding. The left side of his head glistened in the firelight . . . When the people drew back they saw that his left ear had been cut off.

In the New Testament, one of those that stood by cut off the ear of a servant of the high priest when Jesus was arrested—Mark 14:47. I also thought of the book, *Ceremony*, where the new style medicine man makes a cut in Tayo's head during one of their sessions. But the medicine man had a purpose. Maybe it was to make the inward wound visible where it could be healed. Or maybe not. The purpose is left unexplained.

Fire Thunder, it turns out, was not Moves Walking's father after all, but a rejected suitor of his mother, Rattling Hail Woman.

The book continues throughout with high drama. Some of the conflicts are fablesque. A woman marries a star. Birds and animals speak. Wangerin writes with exuberance and passion. His words fly like so many starlings at dusk.

I went back and forth at times thinking I saw shared images from the book of Revelation and from *Black Elk Speaks*, even to the small details of the talking porcupines and the bleeding lips. Wangerin seems to mix faith with the native stories and beliefs. I kept thinking of it as a story mediated by something else, told by someone outside the native culture who yet discerned the issues.

THE SUN DANCE

The Crying for a Vision is a work of fiction, but there are two sections of nonfiction: "Before the Story" as the novel begins, and "Recalling the Sun Dance," an afterword in which Wangerin talks about his trip to the Sun Dance near Rosebud, South Dakota, and his process of research and writing. It is a weaving of fiction, actual experience, and Indian legends. From that experience, Wangerin wrote his story.

A May 29, 2000, review in *Publishers Weekly* states,

> Wangerin's epic account of a boy's sacrifice to save a
> Native American nation from the aftermath of a near-
> apocalyptic war works both as myth and as a story of
> the Lakota people. Moves Walking, a young orphan
> with mysterious spiritual powers, is ostracized for his
> reluctance to learn hunting and battle skills. Ulti-
> mately, however, he must use his gifts to combat the
> blood lust of the warrior Fire Thunder. Maddened
> by unequalled love for Rattling Hail Woman (who
> becomes the wife of a star in the sky), Fire Thunder
> leads the Lakota nation into a tragic war with the
> Crow. Wangerin powerfully conveys the spirit beliefs
> and traditions of the Lakota as he unfolds this stirring
> adventure.

The Crying for a Vision draws on the Lakota belief of
the White Buffalo Calf Woman who came to the Lakota
as a buffalo to present to them their need for a savior. She
appears to two men, one with evil thoughts, the other
willing to listen. The one with the evil thoughts does
not survive the encounter. This reminded me of the two
natures of the Christian believer. Moves Walking himself is caught between good and evil.

Often I saw this book as an eschatological exploration. A spiritual adventure radiating outward from the
culture to a universal territory in the same way *Black
Elk Speaks* reaches beyond the immediate culture to an
"afterworld" landscape. It is a place where stories come

together to talk of eternal matters far beyond any individual culture.

⬦

The Crying for a Vision is also *bildungsroman* in style, a growing-up story. As the novel progresses, Moves Walking has a vision of a star that wants to speak to him. He tries to draw his tribe to the lake where she will appear, but they deride him. A man, Standing Hollow Horn, is especially mocking. But Moves Walking goes to the lake, and his vision broadens. "Behind her there trailed a long cloud of twinkling dust, countless stars, a host of small stars flying hither." Fire Thunder intrudes once. "An entire band of Lakota had become mere shadows on the ground." The beautiful star ascended and the other stars went with her.

Moves Walking, or Waskn Mani, waits for the star to return. His grandmother brings him moccasins and a hunting knife and warns of a gopher that shoots porcupine quills. He goes on a journey and comes to a place of scorched earth. And as he travels into the dark, he comes to the top of the world. There are many voices calling. This calls to mind the main character from *Black Elk Speaks* talking to the grandfathers in his vision.

The star returns from a journey to find a field of bones where she had slept and dreamed.

So *Waskn Mani*, the Lakota boy lying on top of the world, opened his eyes, and lo: there, so close to him that the back of her hand caressed his face, was the loveliest maiden he had ever seen, young and dark and smooth, dressed in white buckskin, smiling sadly, but smiling directly into his gaze. He started to stand up. Fixed on her forehead was a fire-white star. Behind her, bobbing up and down in order each to see him, were a hundred children also smiling. All with lesser stars on their foreheads, a floating host of starchildren.

She tells him they are ghosts trying to find a form to get back into the world. "We were children in a village in which someone committed terrible sin. But no one would confess that he had done it so the entire village was condemned to die, even the innocent." The star asks him to think up a body for them.

"The Great Spirit promised that if one would sacrifice himself we might go home again. All we need is a form for the earth, a body the earth can abide." This is the very heart of the biblical story of Christ coming to earth to save his people. Wangerin does well to hang his story on this, or so it seems to me.

⎯⎯ ∞ ⎯⎯

Wangerin, with his elaborate and ever-flowering prose, tells the story of Fire Thunder who killed Moves Walking's mother and the mothers of the star children without cause. Is it not Satan who was described in the first chapter of Job as creeping around the earth seeking whom he can destroy? And there is a battle in *The Crying for a Vision* nearly equal to that in the Book of Revelation.

The discussions of the existence of sin and of what must be done to remediate are central to the book for me. Along with *Black Elk Speaks*, *The Crying for a Vision* is tied together in the same act of telling our story of redemption. It is my take on the book, anyway. My prism. The point of view through which I see. My bite of the sun.

———⊗———

Shunkmanitu Tanka, a female wolf escaping evil, explains the sacred hoop and tells an old tale. With wisdom such as "every creature on earth appointed to serve another," she continues:

> Once upon a time, our ancestor, the White Wolf, swallowed the sun. He had been a mighty fighter, a glorious hunter by whom the whole people of wolves were satisfied. But he grew proud in his greatness and decided he needed the sun for himself alone. . . . The White Wolf leaped higher than heaven and swallowed the sun. Then the whole world suffered dark and cold and misery. Winter. The circle was broken. Every creature went hungry and none could serve another. That was the black road, *Waskn Mani*, where everyone is for himself with little rules of his own.

(Everyone did that which was right in their own eyes—
Judges 21:25.)

When Moves Walking asked what happened next,
the wolf answers,

> That which must always happen after such a sin.
> Someone died.
>
> *Waskn Mani* gaped. "Who died? . . . How?"
>
> Well, if the hoop is not repaired everyone dies.
> This is the end of the world. But the hoop may be
> repaired if someone will give his life for the sin. The
> one who committed the sin may die unwillingly and
> that is punishment. Or another may choose willingly
> to give his life so that all the people might live. That
> is sacrifice. . . .
>
> "Who died, *Shunkmanitu Tanka*? How?"
>
> The wolf crossed her forepaws on the ground and
> paused. She laid her long chin upon the joint of the
> upper paw.
>
> Punishment, *Waskn Mani*, she said softly. The
> great warrior, the great hunter, our ancestor, died.
> It was in the nature of his sin, for the sun burned
> through his back and cast his corpse to the earth
> where it is lying even today. The White Wolf is the
> frozen snows of the north. Nothing grows from his
> old flesh. He is a dazzling deadness.

The wolf then says they must go hunting.

> "Hunting! . . . To kill? Isn't this what we've been
> talking about? Won't killing break the circle?". . .

Watch me! Watch me, *Waskn Mani*! Taking must break the circle but giving will strengthen it. Giving is serving. Watch me and learn that the sacred hunter asks for the life of her prey—

The wolf continues, "Murder takes a life but hunting receives that life as a gift and so the circle is made stronger." "

The buffalo cow murmured, *Huh! Huh!* She knew. She was not ignorant even in the instant of her death. Softly she said, *Huh!* And then she died. . . . After she [the wolf] bestirred herself and ate and was satisfied by the meat, the wolf sat back on her haunches and sang to the sky. She sang the praise of *Pte* who had given herself with such glory away. Then she sang an invitation, first to the raven and then to others. Come! Come! . . . She called wolverines and buzzards and magpies, coyotes, even the tiny vole. . . . This was the *otuhan*, the give-away.

But the buffalo fought for her life.

No, corrected the wolf. She didn't fight the dying; she fought the wolf. "It is not the hunt that is sinful but the manner of hunting. Ask the hunted."

"If the hoop is not repaired, . . . everyone dies. This is the end of the world. But the sacred hoop may be repaired when someone gives his life for the sin—either in punishment or in sacrifice." This is the wisdom at the core of the book. The wisdom of the believer.

Later, the wolf, *Shunkmanitu Tanka,* launches herself at the throat of Fire Thunder's pony, "ripping the arteries by the bite and slash of her fangs. The pony came down on its right shoulder and pondered surprise for a moment, then lay its head upon the earth and died."

> Fire Thunder had sprung to his feet with a knife in one hand, a spear in the other, and had started toward Moves Walking. The wolf spun round from the pony, barked a warning behind the man and charged. In a smooth feint he sank sideways to one knee, turned, and just as she flew over him he thrust his knife up into her belly. Her weight pitched her into a somersault. Her intestines spilled out. The boy began to wail. The one-eyed warrior rose to his feet and continued toward the wailing boy.

The novel is an amazing, fantastic world full of heightened prose with equally heightened messages.

We are all one. We are all related. We are not separate. We live in a mystifying world. Stars and animals talk. Rabbits attended the birth of Moves Walking. There are animal transformations. Experienced wisdom such as "life and death and life again in a valiant exchange. This, visible, was the circle of the world. This was hunting, *lela wakan,* very holy. With a steadfast gaze the wolf was asking for the life of her prey."

﹡﹡﹡

At best, we can only handle a token bite of the sun. It is these pieces, or bites, that the novel offers. If only we could see native history as it was. It would add to America's understanding of itself.

﹡﹡﹡

Often a story is about something other than itself. In the Old Testament, Nathan tells David the story of a rich man with a flock of sheep and a poor man with only one lamb. When a traveler came, the rich man was not willing to prepare a lamb of his own, but took the one lamb of the poor man and dressed it for the traveler. David is angry and vows revenge on the rich man until Nathan tells him, "You are the man!"—2 Samuel 12:7. Of course, it's the story of David and Bathsheba.

Later, when Absalom is trying to ascend to the throne of his father, he hires a woman to tell David a story: "A handmaid had two sons, and they strove in a field and one smote the other. The whole family asks for the son that murdered the other, that they may kill him and not leave to my husband neither name nor remainder on the earth" —2 Samuel 14:7. David told her to bring the son to him and he would protect him. She answered him, "Why have you thought such a thing against the people of God? For the king does not bring home his banished son, Absalom."

David forgives Absalom, who still works to replace his father until he is killed riding a donkey under a tree where he catches his head between the branches of the oak.

The New Testament has its own parables, most of them spoken by Jesus himself.

❖

There are others who have seen their own meaning in *The Crying for a Vision*. This bite of the sun is from the website *The Art of Reading* by Marianna McComb.

Well, "I am no prophet" but this novel is certainly a great enough matter to leave the dramatic imagery to the professionally published. And rightfully so; Wangerin certainly has his way with dramatic story-telling in *The Crying for a Vision*.

Wangerin's story-telling voice is strong throughout this epic tale of the Lakota people. Wangerin is not overt or conspicuously "Christian" in his narrative, but it is not hard to see how Christ has already written His story within these people's legends. What struck me most while reading is Wangerin's strength in creating images, without being long-winded. His words are concise, powerful, and dramatically captivating. As I read it was not difficult to imagine a movie adaptation playing in my mind. I could see every bit of the story in my mind's eye.

Certain portions of the story are revealed anachronically, while the main narrative moves forward fluidly. While there is much to say about *The Crying for a Vision*, I will focus on one portion of the story that struck me most, though I was greatly moved throughout.

To be sure not to give away any spoilers I'll just say that a woman named Wsu Sna Win (Rattling Hail Woman) leaves her tribe and travels into the mountains where she falls in love with a star named Wicahpi and they are married. They have many happy days together, Wangerin writes. But as a star, his nights are for the sky, to guide the people below. Wsu Sna Win is content for some time, but begins to strive for the love of her husband, which she had already captivated, "so she set herself yet more difficult tasks.... She made a parfleche bag in which he could carry the wasna with him for his nighttime journeys—and on that bag she painted pictures of her home below so that he might account her worthy therefore."

Wicahpi, however, has no earthly need and though he cherishes her efforts and never rejects her gifts: "Oh what delight he expressed for each of these gifts! He grinned and applauded and hugged his mortal wife and wore the leggings all day long.... But every evening when he kissed her and prepared to go eastward he removed the leggings. He never carried the parfleche bag away with him." Wichpi has no use for a wife in the manner which she understands the role of a wife to be from her people. He has no essential need of her for his own existence and purpose as a star. He loves her because he loves her and nothing less. Wsu Sna Win cannot accept this unconditional love, which leads to a break in communion with her husband and a great sadness comes upon her as her sins parallel that of Eve. Even as Wicahpi shared all he was able in love, Wsu Sna Win still clung to her pride and selfish need for Wicahpi to depend on her absolutely.

This immediately stirred me on to meditate on my own relationship with God. There is nothing I have that He needs. If He had need of anything He would not tell me. He does not need me to do anything on his behalf when it comes down to it. How willing am I to accept this? . . . How do I still strive for it? Am I content to be Mary sitting at Jesus feet?

In my own vision of the book, I understand that I am caught between the Joabs, the evil ones, the old Cyclops, Fire Thunder, patterned after Satan himself, and all the characters or situations that those characters become, but as a believer, I have the hope, intercession, and transformative powers of Christ. I understand that Christianity is another form of syncretism, not mixing evil and good, but having to exist with both because the believer finds himself belonging to spirit as well as flesh. Sometimes the Joabs come from within. "O miserable man that I am," said the Apostle Paul, trying to live in the believer's world.

It is the core of the story that holds the power that continues after the book is closed. Are not these stories spider webs that reflect the shape of our world and its truth? That truth, to me, is that Jesus is the Word telling God's story.

Lame Deer, a Sioux holy man, explains the vision quest in Richard Erdoes' *Crying for a Dream: The World through Native American Eyes*:

> Crying for a vision, that's the beginning of all religion. The thirst for a dream from above, without this you are nothing. This I believe. It is like the prophets in your Bible, like Jesus fasting in the desert, getting his visions. It's like our Sioux vision quest, the *hanblecheya*. White men have forgotten this. God no longer speaks to them from a burning bush. If he did, they wouldn't believe it, and call it science fiction.
>
> Your old prophets went into the desert crying for a dream and the desert gave it to them. But the white men today have made a desert of their religion and a desert within themselves. The White Man's desert is a place without dreams or life. There nothing grows. But the spirit water is always way down there to make the desert green again.

Native American literature is a fallen world. What was is no longer. The native world was captured, put into a strange shape not its own, and it has had to learn to adapt and re-create meaning in a new way through stories of the oral tradition transformed into the written word. There also are many forms of syncretism that combine European and traditional ways.

I have been in native churches where a blanket and

peace pipe lay upon the altar. Instead of an organ, there was a drum. There were other symbols. For the Plains Indian, the geometric shapes. For Woodland Indian, the floral. And there was a Bible with the generative substance of its words.

It is unfortunate that re-creation has taken destructive forms such as alcoholism and drug use that at first mimic the holy ways. For a while anyway. But substance abuse is a type of the one-eyed Fire Thunder. Those habits soon collapse into their origin, which is the power and darkness of hell. It is the other side of the spider web, which also captures insects. Again, the oppositional forces at work in the same unit.

Still, God used a small, overlooked being—the word—to create our world, and to speak into his son his mission to catch all of us who would let ourselves be caught in his glorious, reflective web. Jesus. Jesus. You are my Lord. I am consumed.

Passages of Faith
Matthew Dickerson

The Book of Sorrows (1985)

The Orphean Passages (1986)

Saint Julian (2003)

REWRITING THE SAME SONG

THE LATE MARK HEARD (1951–1992), a little-known but brilliant American songwriter, once commented to his friend and fellow songwriter Pat Terry, "I've been writing the same song for twenty-five years. They're all the same. Yeah, you just listen to all my songs. They're just the same songs written over and over in different ways." There is certainly hyperbole in this statement. Heard was a prolific songwriter who wrote and recorded thirteen albums of original work and composed many more songs that were never recorded in a studio. And yet his statement is worth noting: a small number of particularly salient themes keep bubbling up in song after song in a career that spanned more than two decades.

What Mark Heard said of himself could also be said of Walter Wangerin Jr. There is one story, in particular, that Wangerin published at least three times. He wrote it first as a fairy tale titled *The Book of Sorrows* (the 1985 sequel to his award-winning novel *The Book of the Dun Cow*). He wrote it again in the pages of *The Orphean Passages* (1986), combining a modern novel about a pastor named Orpheus, a retelling of the Greek myth of Orpheus and Eurydice, and a sermon on faith. He published the story yet a third time as a medieval romance titled *Saint Julian* (2003). If you count his retelling of the Greek myth of Orpheus, then Wangerin told the story four times: as myth, as fairy tale, as medieval romance, and as modern novel.

Of course these four stories are also distinct, each unique in its own right, just as Mark Heard's songs vary in melody, chord structure, rhythm, harmony, and imagery even when sharing a common theme. A work of art—whether story, song, poem, or painting—must not be reduced to an abstract message or theme. A story doesn't merely *contain* characters, setting, concrete images, word choices, and plot; a story *is* those things. *Saint Julian* is thus a different novel than *The Orphean Passages*, which is different from *The Book of Sorrows*. We do injustice to the story and storyteller when we reduce story to message and when we confuse a novel with a sermon. Walt Wangerin Jr. was a great storyteller; he understood the value of story *as story* as well as anybody.

Mark Heard himself, despite what he said in private self-deprecating conversation about repeatedly rewriting the same song, often bemoaned how reducing a song to a mere message devalues art and song. In the liner notes of one of his early albums, he discussed this in the context of Platonic Gnosticism.

> When couched in the terminology of the Christian subculture, this thought may find its way into teaching in a form like, "A song is not to be appreciated. Only that which it expresses (the goodness of God, for example) can be appreciated as having value and justifying the existence of the song. The melody and the poetry are irrelevant and insignificant." This is a low view of creativity and a low view of the Creation. How sad that the beauty God has created as well as latent beauty expressible through human hands and voices cannot be appreciated. How sad to wish a bird would preach rather than sing.

So to say in a reductionist way that he had repeatedly rewritten the same song because there is a message it expresses would miss the significance and relevance of melody, poetry, and all the other artistic aspects that make it a song.

Heard's use of "sing" is particularly fitting. For, as James Schaap noted in an earlier chapter, Walter

ter.

Wangerin was (metaphorically speaking) a pastor who sang. His vocation was preaching. But he didn't preach *rather* than sing. His preaching was singing. His singing was preaching.

But his singing was also still singing. That is, his stories were also still stories.

THE BOOK OF SORROWS: TRUTH IN MYTH, FAIRY, AND STORY

Stories, like songs, cannot be reduced to a platitude or truth. And yet they contain profound truth. At least the better ones do. Thus, Wangerin can say that his character Orpheus, "though unique, is at the same time one among a countless throng which includes you and me, each unique as well." Pastor Orpheus is unique, and his story is unique. Yet a countless throng of fellow travelers in this fallen world share a common experience, living lives resembling his story, though in different ways and at different times. It is appropriate, therefore, that Wangerin has retold these different stories—this one story—in different ways, yet with each retelling incarnating a similar underlying truth.

For even stories that take the form of myth—a word our modern culture unfortunately often uses synonymously with lie—contain truth. Indeed, according to Wangerin, myths *especially* contain truth. He wrote in the introduction to *The Orphean Passages,*

In order to comprehend the experience one is living in, he must, by imagination and by intellect, be lifted out of it. He must be given to see it whole; but since he can never wholly gaze upon his own life while he lives it, he gazes upon the life that, in symbol, comprehends his own. Art presents such lives, such symbols. Myth especially—persisting as a mother of truth through countless generations and for many disparate cultures, coming therefore with the approval not of a single people but of *people*—myth presents, myth *is*, such a symbol, shorn and unadorned, refined and true. And when the one who gazes upon that myth suddenly, in dreadful recognition, cries out, "There I am! That is me!" then the marvelous translation has occurred: he is lifted out of himself to see himself wholly.

Wangerin does just this, through myth, fairy tale, romance, and modern novel. His stories, if we are willing to gaze at them, lift us up out of our own experiences so that we can turn around and see those experiences more wholly and clearly. We can see truth. We comprehend, finally. Except if that truth is difficult to see, we may need to see it in many ways, in many stories. Or many versions of the same story, as it were.

So what is this story that continues to resurface in different forms—that keeps bubbling up from Wangerin's creative and pastoral imagination? At the simplest level, it is a story of one who must pass through utter devastation, loss, and brokenness before being able, finally, to taste and accept God's grace and goodness.

The story tells of the passages in our journeys of faith when we cannot hear the voice of the One in whom we have put that faith, when we do not experience His presence. Wangerin writes in the sermon embedded in *The Orphean Passages* that such a silent passage is inevitable in every faith journey: "Faith leads, if it doesn't deviate its proper course, to pain and unspeakable pain." And so he tells us the story of that unspeakable pain, because he believes it is an inevitable part of the faith journey. He tells us also of the grace that follows.

The first version of this story comes to us in *The Book of Sorrows*, the sequel to *The Book of the Dun Cow*. What kind of stories are these Dun Cow novels? The great fantasy writer and Oxford philologist J. R. R. Tolkien once described his motives for writing *The Lord of the Rings* and his Middle-earth *Legendarium*, saying that he set out to create for England "a body of more or less connected legend, ranging from the large and cosmogonic, to the level of romantic fairy-story—the larger founded on the lesser in contact with the earth, the lesser drawing splendor from the vast backclothes." Wangerin seems to have incorporated all of these elements into the Dun Cow stories. These tales contain elements of cosmic myth, elements of romantic fairy-tale, and elements of heroic fantasy.

Of the three books addressed in this chapter, Wangerin published *The Book of Sorrows* first. It remains my favorite: one of the most profoundly beautiful and moving stories of brokenness and grace I have ever read. Yet those who set out to read the book should also know that it is aptly titled. It is a tale full of sorrow, and one I do not often reread. I wouldn't pick it up for a quick Sunday evening read as I might do with one of Lewis's Narnia stories. It requires tremendous emotional energy to engage it as it needs to be engaged, to enter into it, to read it from the inside. Though the tale ends in joy, healing, and forgiveness, the path to that joy leads through pain and loss.

The Book of Sorrows is about a pastor of sorts: a rooster named Chauntecleer. Chauntecleer leads a flock of animals engaged in a great and horrible war against the demonic Wyrm. Though his flock begins (in *The Book of the Dun Cow*) with only the animals from his own barnyard, as the war rages, refugees arrive from other distant barnyards and woodlands and riverbanks. They come together under the care of the rooster Chauntecleer, who loves them and wants desperately to protect them, and so takes their burdens upon himself. He assumes this task: to gather his growing flock under his wings, to lead the war against Wyrm and defeat him in order to save those under his care.

But the rooster is not able to bear that burden. As told in *The Book of the Dun Cow*, he was barely able to defeat Wyrm's captain, Cockatrice. He is no match for Wyrm himself. Wyrm is defeated, but not by Chauntecleer, and not without terrible devastation and loss.

Because he could not protect them, many of his flock, including the rooster's own sons, are killed—casualties of the war.

Chauntecleer cannot bear that those he loved suffered and died at the hands of evil and that he could not protect them. And where was God through all of his suffering? Why was God silent? Why did He allow this? Chauntecleer also cannot bear the fact that the power and grace of the Dun Cow and the sacrifice of a lowly dog named Mundo Cani—a dog whom Chauntecleer had despised for his humble state—ultimately defeated Wyrm: that his own strength and determination had proven insufficient. He cannot bear that Mundo Cani died *in his place*: that he, the rooster, couldn't protect the dog. *The Book of Sorrows* begins shortly after this war has ended. Chauntecleer is grieving and angry. Angry at God. Angry also at himself. He begins to beat his own body. "I'll go to the end, the *end*!" he exclaims as he strikes his own crop in an act of self-flagellation. "'And why? Because I could not,' he hissed with ruinous emotion: 'Because I could not save my Mundo Cani.'"

Thus Chauntecleer sets his own course. For there is this, also: only the *body* of Wyrm was defeated; Wyrm himself—the spirit of Wyrm, the *evil* of Wyrm—lives on.

Yes. Wyrm is alive. Chauntecleer knows because he hears Wyrm's voice. But the dog is dead. And because the dog is dead, Chauntecleer in his pride is unable to forgive himself, or to accept the grace and forgiveness of the Dun Cow. For the dog had accomplished what Chauntecleer himself wanted to accomplish, and so the rooster's pride mingles with his despair. Pride feeds on despair. And in that pride, Chauntecleer causes sorrow upon sorrow as he desperately seeks some great "Something to do" that will prove his worthiness: an act that will earn his forgiveness. "WYRM!" he cries out eight times near the start of the story. "WYRM, I WILL KILL YOU FOR WHAT YOU HAVE DONE TO ME!" Thus he ultimately settles on a two-fold act to make himself worthy: going himself to the Netherworld, recovering the bones of Mundo Cani Dog from the rotting corpse of Wyrm, and killing Wyrm a second time. "I MYSELF WILL KILL THE EVIL ONE, AND I WILL SET THE GOOD ONE FREE!" he proclaims.

Once he decides on this course, the progression is inexorable. He embarks on another war of sorts, makes another attempt to defeat evil in order to assuage his guilt and purify himself. But he can no more purify himself than he can defeat evil by himself. He has not learned the lesson of his pride, despite his protestations—"I'm a very wise Rooster," he claims—and so he becomes responsible for more death: the deaths of the coyotes Rachel and her son Benoni, the beloved wife and child of an insecure and fearful coyote named Ferric. Woe to the reader, however, for these deaths take place only after Wangerin has invited us to love this foolish and fearful, loving and loveable coyote Ferric: a coyote who, despite his deep-seated insecurity and insufficiency, also deeply loves his wife and his three children whom he must watch starve during the horrible winter that follows the first death of Wyrm: a coyote who has the same number of children as Chauntecleer lost in the war. But whereas it was Wyrm's servants, the basilisks, who were responsible for the deaths of Chauntecleer's children, it is Chauntecleer himself, in his foolish quest to rescue the already-dead dog in his self-righteous rage against Wyrm, who is responsible for the deaths of Ferric's kin, Rachel his wife and Benoni Coyote his child.

Thus another guilt is added to the rooster's burden. After struggling mightily to serve heaven in a deserving way, Chauntecleer finally decides that "Heaven is empty." Empty, or perhaps just silent, which might be even worse.

Slowly the rooster-pastor becomes a ruthless dictator. Perhaps to make up for his own lack of perfection, he demands legalistic perfection from his flock. And he distrusts them all. He hurts the ones he loves, those who have served him most faithfully, even those who continue to love him selflessly. Because he thought he could defeat evil by himself—and failed—he becomes self-righteous and self-vindicating, and eventually altogether denies both evil and the God whom he believes is silent, the God who would not defeat evil the way Chauntecleer wanted. So the rooster becomes a loner, with the whole world his enemy.

Even his most loyal follower, John Wesley Weasel, understands this and confronts him.

> "Rooster, he *kills* that baby. He kill's baby's mama too!"
>
> Chauntecleer staggers. The naked indictment hits him like a rock, the personal sin that he had refused to know; and for an instant the Cock is vulnerable, hanging on the air.

That indictment and guilt is not enough, however, to bring repentance. For Chauntecleer is "armed with convictions now that shield him from guilt: there is no sin. There is no sin in all the bloody world." And so the "Rooster seems only to swell into a grand nobility, solitary before the forces ranged against him, and unafraid."

Chauntecleer must fall to the absolute bottom before he is able to see his need, abandon his pride, and accept forgiveness. The forgiveness comes from the bereaved coyote Ferric. From his wife Pertelote. From God.

When Ferric comes to the rooster, he comes not for revenge as Chauntecleer imagines, but to forgive. And to love. "I love you, Chanty-clear," he repeats over and over, while the rooster wounds him. And "See? I forgive you."

Only then is Chauntecleer broken. Broken by love. "The Rooster has delivered himself to grief. He is gulping the air and sobbing like an infant. His tears drill the dirty snow." And then he cries out. "Oh, God! Oh, God! Oh, dear God." And he knows, again, that there is evil. The evil has been inside himself all along. The evil of pride. The evil of thinking that he, alone, could defeat evil. In the love and forgiveness of a lowly coyote, heaven speaks.

This is Walter Wangerin's story: the protagonist who must fall to the very bottom, and then fall even further. A protagonist who goes through what Wangerin calls a *silent passage*—a time when God is not speaking to him. A protagonist who, in a prideful desire to be worthy of God's love and to do God's work, cannot experience or accept grace. Only through complete and utter brokenness does that protagonist finally experience and taste love and grace.

The Orphean Passages:
Drama, Story, and Song of Faith

The Orphean Passages is also a story about a pastor. Not a rooster in a mythical landscape, but a human living in our modern world. Should we be surprised that two stories by a pastor about a pastor have much in common? That they would be the same?

This modern-day pastor is named Orpheus. Like Chauntecleer the rooster, Orpheus has a deep love for God and a desire to serve God in a holy way and to serve God's people as well. It is *not* a story about a prodigal who can't hear God because he has chosen a selfish life of hedonistic pleasure; those are the villains of literature we identify much too easily, because they are somebody *else*. Rather, it is a story of somebody who wants desperately to be holy and unselfish. He has tasted of God's love, and he loves God back.

Orpheus is thirteen years old when he is confirmed, and on his confirmation day, he commits his life to God. "Orpheus willingly enacted his love for Jesus that day," the narrator tells us. And again, a little bit later, the narrator repeats this refrain. "Thirteen-year-old Orpheus loved Jesus long; . . . He loved him deeply, as deep as mysteries." The story suggests no lack of sincerity in this love. There is no hint of rebellion. The words speak of a love for Jesus as deep as a childlike heart can feel. So why would such a sincere and childlike heart need to go through utter despair and a sense of abandonment by God before he can taste grace?

In the sermon that accompanies this novel, Wangerin writes about faith as a verb: something we *do* rather than something we *have*. He also writes about faith as a constantly changing action that inevitably goes through various passages. Thus the title of the book contains the word "passages." Thus the subtitle of this book is *The Drama of Faith*.

One passage of faith—unavoidable, Wangerin claims—is the "silent passage": the time when God does not speak to us in any voice we can hear. And because we do not hear God, we believe he has abandoned us. In our anguish at God's silence or abandonment, we lose our faith; we rebel against the very one whose voice we so desperately want to hear.

This is, indeed, the Greek story of Orpheus, the son of Apollo—a myth retold by Virgil, Ovid, and others. In the myth, it is not God who is silent, but rather Orpheus' dead lover Eurydice. Orpheus has descended into the Netherworld, the realm of Hades, to rescue her. Does this tale sound familiar? In *The Book of Sorrows*, we saw echoes of it in Chauntecleer's journey into the Netherworld to rescue the dead dog that loved him. But Orpheus, unlike the rooster, is offered a living lover. All he needs to do is ascend the stair back to the realm of the living and Eurydice will follow him. Yet he must do it without turning around, without making sure that she is behind him. This uncertainty and silence causes the tremendous anguish. Does each step he takes up the stairs from the underworld bring him closer to reunion with Eurydice, or farther away? This is the silent passage of the Orpheus of Greek myth. When the hero fears that his beloved is no longer with him, he commits the faithless act that causes him to lose her forever; he does what the god Hades has forbidden, and turns and looks at her, thus dooming her.

Pastor Orpheus will go through that silent passage also. Like his Greek namesake, and like the rooster, he will descend into his own Netherworld. Wangerin's book—which contains a sermon on faith, a modern novel, and a retelling of the ancient Greek myth—is in part an exploration of the inevitability of that silent passage. Wangerin interrupts the singing of his story with the singing of his sermon, and in the sermon, he explains that faith is a verb and not a noun; faith is not something we *have*—rather, *faithing* is something we *do*. Because it is not static, but moving, active, alive, it will go through changes and passages. It is important to understand this, Wangerin explains, because one of those passages is this silent passage, when heaven does not speak to us and in our anguish we cry out against God in rage or rebellion.

> When the relationship between the Lord and us is troubled; when we, like Jeremiah, spit against the Deity; or when we cry, as surely we will in the deep sincerity of our souls, "There is no God!" then, if all we had for definition were the noun *faith*, we would have to judge ourselves faith-less, fallen from the faith, cast out. And that were the worst of deaths to die. On the other hand, if it is faithing which we are experiencing, and if this desolated cry arises from one scene in a long and fluid play, then even the desolation may have its place in the changing relationship, caused by previous action, causing actions subsequent; then despair may be an episode in the drama. And then we are not fallen from the faith, but rather falling within it—and even this, dear child, may be *of* the faith.

Despair and desolation are part of Pastor Orpheus's story, as they are of Chauntecleer's. Wangerin tells the story again, however, so that readers understand that it need not be about despair *only*, but also hope and grace.

There is another thread here as well that weaves through all versions of the story, making them many but also one. Or, we might say, there is another hint about why Pastor Orpheus finds himself in this silent passage. What previous action led to that despair and desolation in the face of a heaven that seemed to have fallen silent?

The answer is part of the central theme in all three books. Readers may see a hint of the theme in the child Orpheus even at the age of thirteen. As Chauntecleer loves his flock and wants to be worthy of their respect, so, too, young Orpheus loves God and wants desperately to be worthy of God's love for him. On the day of his confirmation, however, despite his love for Jesus and his desire to look beautiful for Jesus, he has a "rooster-tail" of hair. Even as we make a connection between Chauntecleer's Netherworld journey and that of the Greek Orpheus, we may also see a connection between this future pastor and the pastor with a more literal rooster tail: a connection between two pastors who both desperately desire to help God defeat evil. In any case, young Orpheus is unable to control his hair. He cannot look as perfect and beautiful for God as he wants to look. And so, even at the age of thirteen, "Orpheus was stricken by unworthiness."

Many years later, Orpheus is a pastor of an inner-city church, another pastor who takes his parishioners under his own wings and seeks in his righteous love to shield them from evil. To defeat evil. To pray so fervently that God himself will come and defeat evil. But there are so many people he can't save. So many he doesn't seem able to help, despite all his efforts. There is Allouise Story. How fervently he prays for her. "*Oh, for the lady's sake, let me prevail*," he prays. "*She needs to know your love.*"

And in praying for her (and so many others) Orpheus is also praying for himself. He needs to know that God hears him, that God not only is there and is loving, but that he, Orpheus, is worthy of that love. His prayer becomes something different: "*For my sake, Lord! I need to see you, dear Lord Jesus! Are you near me?*"

Despite all his praying, however, her problems do not go away. Is Orpheus not doing enough? Not praying hard enough? Not a good enough person? Or, he wonders later, is it because he is doing what he is doing for himself and not for her. Thus, his sense of his own unworthiness is compounded further. "I am guilty of this woman," he confesses.

And there is Corie Jones and his trouble with the law. And Arabelle Lee and her trouble with men. And Dolores Johnson who loves Orpheus and who is loved by Orpheus, which also makes Orpheus feel guilty.

Here again is that proverbial rooster-tail. The pride of a rooster. The shame of a thirteen-year-old boy. How our pride and our shame go hand in hand. Orpheus wants to be worthy, but he isn't. Rather than accepting his own unworthiness and the grace and love that come with it, he beats himself up. *"I belong in Hell,"* he tells himself. And because he knows he doesn't deserve kindness, he can't accept that either. Not even the kindness of Dolores, who loves him. Especially not that kindness. *"Kindness hurts me,"* he cries out. For he doesn't deserve it. And he wants to deserve the love he receives.

As in the tale of Chauntecleer, Orpheus loses everything, falls to the bottom, and then falls further. When Orpheus is declared "ex-pastor" and "ex-man," when his health is broken and everything has been taken away, even the love of Dolores, when he stops thinking he must be the one to help everybody—only then does he taste grace. He becomes not the minister who solves the world's problems by ministering to others, but the one to whom others minister: the one who accepts the ministering of others. And those others are the members of his flock who had seemed most beyond his help. As with *The Book of Sorrows*, this is where the tale ends. There can be no other way, Wangerin tells us. "In this broken world, given the characters we bring unto the drama, it had to be. We go through death to meet our Jesus, wholly to love him, wholly to be possessed by the love of him."

Saint Julian

I began writing this chapter more than a year before I finished it. I have written entire books in less time than it took me to finish this one chapter-length essay. It was not that I started out slowly. I quickly finished a first draft of my introduction as well as the section on *The Book of Sorrows*. The Dun Cow stories are books I know well, have thought carefully about for years, and have written about elsewhere. I also reread *The Orphean Passages*—another book I have often quoted—took notes, and soon outlined my section on that story.

Then I stalled. Weeks turned into months. I had no end of excuses: important deadlines for my own fantasy novel and for another work of creative nonfiction, grading student papers at the college where I teach, preparing and teaching my classes, travel and speaking. Then washing dishes, checking social media for messages. Changing light bulbs. Really, any excuse served.

I delayed finishing the chapter for more than a year because I was afraid of rereading *Saint Julian*. I did not want to reenter the pain and sorrow of the story, despite how beautifully Wangerin tells it. Perhaps not even despite how beautifully the story is told, but *because* of how beautifully it is told. A poorly-told story would not move me enough to draw a deep emotional response. But such a carefully-crafted novel—such a well-told story, a vividly-painted work of art, a beautiful song—cannot help but pull readers in. When I finally came around to rereading the novel, I discovered I was not wrong about either the beauty of the writing or about the sorrow of the reading. I also understood why I think of this book in a different way than the other two.

Saint Julian is Wangerin's retelling of the medieval tale of Saint Julian the Hospitaller, who is the patron saint of travelers and a renowned hunter. It can also be understood as a rewriting of *The Book of Sorrows* or *The Orphean Passages*. The central threads of Julian's story are very similar to those of the other books. As with *The Book of Sorrows*, sorrows fill the tale; "Sorrows" is the title of the fourth part.

In the thirteenth-century version of the story of Saint Julian, written by a Dominican priest named Giacomo da Varazze, Julian is cursed by witches when he is born. The curse is that he will one day kill both of his parents. This prophecy brings to mind the Greek tragedy of Oedipus in both kind and scale—a prophecy or curse that cannot be escaped. When Julian learns of that curse, to protect his parents from himself, he gives up his very inheritance and flees his home. However, his flight does not prevent the tragedy.

Wangerin's version varies slightly, keeping the same tragic trajectory, but replacing the witch with a great stag. From a young age, Julian is a supernaturally-gifted archer. Though he does not have the strength and stature of his father, and is judged too weak to be a knight and go off to war, his eyes and hands move faster than seems humanly possible. He needs only to see something move, and he can have an arrow nocked to the bow in the flash of an eye. His arrows do not miss. And because he delights in his skill, he learns also to delight in hunting and killing. Or perhaps it is the other way around: because he delights in hunting, he learns to revel in his skill—to hear the rhythm of the woods and to sense all living things around him.

On the day before he is to be knighted by the king, Julian goes on a daylong hunting rampage, indiscriminately slaughtering every animal in the forest, leaving their corpses to rot. This action dooms his father's fiefdom, because its people depend on the wild animals for food during the winter. It also dooms Julian himself. The last animal he kills is a great stag, which he shoots after killing every other deer in the herd. "And the stag said, *Juuuuuu-lian, thou art cursed.*" And what is that curse? "The great stag, dreadfully rampant, cried: *As thou hast taken the lives of the forest, so shalt thou kill thy mother dead.*" And then, again, "*And as thou hast murdered me, my son, so shalt thou murder thy father and thy lord!*" By whose power is the stag speaking the language of men? The narrator does not tell us. But upon hearing the words "my son," readers may wonder: Is this the voice of Julian's heavenly father? Of God himself?

Julian tells no one of these words. But then he has two near accidents, one in which he narrowly misses killing his mother with an arrow, and another in which he narrowly misses killing his father by knocking a battle ax off the wall above his throne. Because he loves his parents deeply, Julian runs away to escape that curse. He disappears from his father's lands and his parents' lives, hides his name, and does all he can to hide from his fate. By his great prowess with a bow and his skill at woodcraft and fieldcraft, he becomes a hero in the wars against the Saracens, killing many enemies. After his victories secure a lasting peace for his king, he marries a woman who loves him deeply. And though still plagued by his past, he seems to settle into a life with at least some moments of happiness.

His parents, however, never gave up loving him or searching for him. Eventually they find him, and the curse overtakes him.

The threads common to the other tales are not difficult to see. Like both Chauntecleer and Pastor Orpheus, Julian has a great desire to be worthy. At first, it is a desire to be worthy of his father's love. It is not the desire of a child who feels unloved and longs for love, but the desire of a child who *is* loved and yet feels unworthy of that love. When his father embraced him, "Julian felt a blaze of shame to seep his cheeks . . . The love of his father was oblivious of Julian's truer self. The one whom his father was embracing could never equal the one whom his father *thought* he was embracing, and Julian suffered the difference all privily within himself alone." But that desire also is, or becomes, a desire to be worthy of any love, especially the love of God. Such a desire is impossible to fulfill. None can be worthy of God's love. The more Julian is aware of his failure, the more desperate he becomes and the more he despises himself for his unworthiness. He loses his will to live. "But Julian lived. And year by year despised himself for living."

Like those pastors from the other stories, this saint also receives great adoration. He is adored first by his father's people, who don't know Julian's thirst for killing, and believe only that the young Julian is a devout young man. Later, after he flees his home and becomes a war leader who slays Saracens by the hundreds, he is praised for both his valor and his piety.

Most importantly, he is loved by his wife—like Chauntecleer and his hen Pertelote. For a time, Julian is able to accept that love. But once he has slain his own parents, thinking them strangers, he cannot accept even his wife's love. His words to her bear a striking resemblance to the words of Pastor Orpheus to Dolores, when he tells her that her kindness hurts. "'Every gesture of love must tear my flesh as if with hooks,' Julian wails, 'for I know I do not deserve your love. Oh, woman, 'tis what *I* am! Love in any form can do nothing but scourge me with the whip-knots of my sin!'" And so he leaves her also, and in his own brokenness, he breaks her as surely as he had broken his own parents. But he does this only after Wangerin has painted a poignant picture of the depths and sincerity and selfless nature of her love for him. Our readers' sorrow is thus deepened.

This sorrow leads readers back to the central thread that runs through all three tales. The hero, completely broken, beyond hope, cannot save himself—when Julian, like Chauntecleer and Orpheus, has reached "Wretched, wordless, desolation," when he cries out his sin before God, then his childhood Almoner returns and speaks: "Heavenly mercy never left thee. Here it hath lain and here it lieth still above thine heart, waiting, waiting for thee so to fail thyself that nothing is left but mercy."

Julian has so failed in *doing* something to make himself worthy, that he knows that no *doing* is possible. "'But what shall I do?' he says. He begs this. It is the very supplication which has tormented him all these latter years; aye, but this time he begs and does not answer it himself. For now he knows he has no answer, and so his begging is pure."

⚬⚬⚬

It was only as I reread this book when writing this chapter that I named what bothered me the first time I read this story. There is a thread in this story I had not seen in the others. And yet in the very naming of that thread that bothered me, I glimpsed something else also—an even deeper thread that answered the first.

Julian was being punished for his sins, and mercy was withheld from him until he had paid the price—first for the slaughter of the animals of the forest, and second for the slaughter of the Saracens. At the end of the story, he finds grace and mercy, but only after he and all who loved him most—his father, his mother, his wife—lost their lives paying for his sins. It is the animals of the forest

that drive Julian into a rage that causes him to unknow-
ingly slay his parents. And again, when he seeks to take
his own life, he has the vision of the animals appearing
in judgment. In the final moment of Julian's life, before
he is taken up to heaven, Christ himself appears in the
form of the traveling leper demanding hospitality from
Julian, and speaks words of judgment. "Thou has murdered me often, hast slain me again and again a thousand
times again."

For it was, indeed, Christ whom Julian killed. Christ
he killed when he slayed the animals and left them to rot.
Christ he killed when he slayed the Saracen shepherd in
his own sheepfold. Christ he was killing in battle after
battle. Was it Christ also who spoke to him through the
stag? Who sent the vision of the animals? For as much
as you have done to the least of His brethren, you have
done to Him.

True enough. But I also wondered where Christ's
mercy was earlier. That seeming lack of mercy troubled
me. If any of us were punished for our sins, we would
all live lives as tragic as Julian's, and still we would not
have paid enough. Thus in this story of Julian's fall to the
very bottom of the pit before discovering grace, I read
also a story of punishment and retribution. This punishment falls not only on Julian, but also on his mother and
father and wife. Where was mercy for them?

The truth is, we cannot know how the father and
mother and wife experienced God's mercy. This is not

their story. It is Julian's. Is it fair that those who loved him suffered for their love? No. But it is the truth. Life is full of such unfair sufferings. Who has not loved deeply and been deeply hurt by that love? Yet life is surely richer because of it—as Julian's story is more beautiful because of the love of Julian's wife and the goodness of his mother and father. In their love, we see reflected the perfect love of Christ, the model of what it means to love to the point of death. It is another pointer within the story to the power of mercy and the cost of mercy.

And in the end, *Saint Julian* is not a story of punishment, but a story of mercy. And I missed just how deep that was. This story also reminds us that all of our sins carry consequences. All of our sins cause suffering for others and in God's creation. All of creation groans.

It was Christ himself who came to Julian in the form of the leper and proclaimed the truth of what Julian had done; it was Christ too who embraced Julian and brought him to his eternal peace. In the closing paragraphs, the narrator sums up the tale: "All his life's laboring was only wrestling. He burned out his little time in wrestling—first with God, and second with himself. But the fight he is leaving behind . . . And Julian's soul is laughing now, as booming and boisterous as the thunder. And the Lord's embrace is his golden rope."

Letters from
the Land of Cancer
Luci Shaw

Letters from the Land of Cancer (2010)

LETTERS FROM THE LAND OF CANCER is a brief book about a large concern. It is about time—the time we have left to live on this planet, each and all of us who are mortal. "Terminal" is the appropriate term, when, in the midst of a full and flourishing life, we are jerked to a halt by something that is bigger than we are, that takes over our lives, our thinking, our plans for the future. The book is about the aggressive shock we feel at the announcement that something over which we have little control is invading our bodies and seeping into our minds and souls.

For many years I have known and admired Walt Wangerin, the friend who wrote these letters out of the extremity of his cancer, describing his progress through the entire dis-easy process of early symptoms, diagnosis, treatment, and resolution. In one letter, he describes his discoveries as "dispatches," as if he has gone ahead of us, to some distant front, and must send back detailed descriptions of what is going on out there, what must be prepared for. Though the themes of cancer and dying may seem unduly morbid to the young and healthy, they can, in this small book, offer an understanding of what matters in life and faith. These themes engaged Wangerin's keen and perceptive mind and, once published as *Letters from the Land of Cancer*, became a source of insight into how we might view the reason for our life, and our life in God, as well as how we can learn to deal with these mysteries.

Having had my own brush with the threat of cancer, I have a personal appreciation of Walt's predicament, a visceral response to the threat of an illness unto death. We, who started our lives as utterly helpless infants, may find ourselves infantile again, giving our very existence over to our caretakers. And, as Wangerin says, we may need to allow ourselves to be comforted, as a baby is comforted: lifted, carried, sung to, rocked in the consoling arms of our parents. And of our Parent. Fed, clothed, blessed by love in the midst of pain and the questions that accompany it. Wangerin's illustration of this dependency, given at the end of a sermon at his Grace Church, is memorable. He puts his thumb in his mouth and sucks it, as a baby will!

This is the practice of mortality.

When Walt first received a diagnosis of cancer, which his physician told him had metastasized to his lymph nodes from somewhere else, he began to document his inner and outer life in the form of letters to his family and friends. He had noticed a swelling in his neck, and after examinations and PET scans, and after becoming acquainted with all the varied arcane devices that penetrate human flesh for discovery, he was informed of his disease. His immediate response, voiced in early letters, was, "This is a new adventure." But we secretly wondered, "Walt, are you and your doctors setting up a new business—*Doctors & Dying, Incorporated*?"

The letters came to us at intervals, as personal, almost chatty stories, informal, as if he were in the room with us. And now, in these printed pages, he speaks to us again with a similar intimacy, but speaks to a wider audience. His reflections may mirror our own, but they extend them and fill them with flesh and spirit. He writes with such disarming spontaneity—sometimes from the chair in his doctor's office as he waits for an appointment—that we feel we are face to face with him. We sense the brush of breath against the cheek as we read his words.

This is how true friendship works: Walt was examining what was happening by way of his self-consciousness and his own pastoral wisdom, and passing on his findings to us, his buddies, his community, in a continuing reportage. At the time, we could not know how long the letters would keep coming.

Walt tends, in his fiction, to a certain idiosyncratic style, almost as if he were writing prophetic messages similar to the proclamations of biblical prophets. These letters are far more informal, more candid and straightforward, and often decorated with snatches of conversation and imagery. Initially, he did not seem to intend these letters to be published. But now, here they are, for our benefit and understanding.

In a sense, he has kept these letters as a journal for himself and us so that his experience wouldn't get lost in a haze of forgetfulness. He expected bodily fatigue, pain, and weakness, but could not know, between each interval of writing, what the disease or the therapies would do to his mind. Or for how long he would be able to express himself coherently. His powers of description have always been invigorating, imaginative, and are spoken into the air and our minds with magisterial authority and insight. His epistles to the community of friendship retain that power. But at the time he was writing them, we all wondered, "For how long?"

VIVID PRESENCE

Walter Wangerin Jr. is a man of vivid presence. His powers of imagination and intelligence have been flashing from his mind and his tongue as long as I've known him. In my imagination, I've always envisioned him as a raven-haired Celtic warrior or an eagle. Not a predatory bird, but one with marine-blue eyes that see far and keenly, whose vision penetrates the landscape of the human condition down to the individual rock or weed. Although never dispassionately or clinically. He also admits, "But I have ever been a man of melancholies." Which links him with the company of the oppressed and anxious. A Lutheran pastor, but also a broadly-known novelist of wide reach and precocious gifts, he has won a multitude of awards. The fact that he also writes passionate poetry (he once sent me an untidy package of typed poems gathered for possible publication) as well as books for young children, developed with a tenderness and understanding drawn from his own fathering, endears him to me.

Years ago, while my own husband was dying of lung cancer—he lived after his diagnosis for eighteen months—I was the one who wrote the journal, not in the form of letters, though there were plenty of those, but as an intentional daily record in a blank notebook that I kept at the ready in my purse. Soon enough, I became familiar with the technical jargon of this whole new medical arena. (Though not a medical provider myself, I come from a family in which all the men are physicians, and I was a fast learner.) The gleanings from this very personal journal were eventually published in my book

God in the Dark, and described our entry into the dark tunnel of cancer. The clot that Harold coughed up, large as a bloody egg, was the first sign of something seriously amiss. The tentative diagnosis was "walking pneumonia." Weeks later, the panicky shortness of breath at midnight caused him to sit up, panting "I can't breathe," and I drove him, speeding, to the local ER where the X-rays showed an opacity on his left lung—an indication that it was filled with fluid. The following day, we visited the local oncologist. As Harold sat on the examining table, the great man said, matter-of-factly, as if he was discussing the weather, "You have lung cancer. You have eighteen months to live." I sat down suddenly. I thought I might faint. The startle of it. We were both undone, paralyzed in mind and spirit.

How was this possible? Harold had never smoked. He was a gifted, gracious, godly man in the prime of life. So why lung cancer? We had a flourishing, young book publishing company going. We had new grandchildren arriving, each an occasion for family joy. Then, without warning, our foreseeable lives came stumbling to a halt at a cliff edge. Were we destined to fly or fall?

The ups and downs—physically, emotionally, spiritually—bewildered us. Every day we woke to questions. What next? What did this mean? What were we to think now about God's purpose for our lives? I began to keep meticulous records of results from scans, blood tests, watching for levels of "cancer markers." A meteorological record of emotional weather. Every new test result was cause for either relief or despair. I noted each of them, not wanting any of this experience to get lost in a blur of forgetting. Everything had significance.

Together we drove regularly from our western suburb to a major medical center in Chicago to meet with our new oncologist, the one who was said to be up on all of the latest cancer therapies. Dr. Kathy was a Christian and it was a relief to realize that she was as eager as we were to test the power of healing prayer along with the radiation and chemo. We began to enlist prayer partners at our church. Dear friends in the Catholic charismatic renewal movement came weekly to intercede with God for us. We called them the friends of the heart.

Soon we also got to know the technicians and nurses at the hospital. They became our caregivers and familiars, but not our friends. I realized that I didn't *want* them to become my friends, as if this situation were normal. This whole unplanned cancer scenario felt ludicrous and the exploration of this vast new territory we had to undertake was an unwelcome experience.

After some months of chemotherapy there was a temporary letup in Harold's pain. The tumors were still there but their growth had been arrested. His labored breathing eased a bit. Some life energy returned, as if the elasticity of a limp rubber band was reviving. We both went back to work at the publishing company. We drove east to Cape Cod for a family vacation replete with sun and sandy beaches and the smell of salt in the air. We ate clam chowder and local lobster. A whole generation of siblings and young cousins gathered. Our children and grandchildren spent days with Harold, a time made even more meaningful because of his illness, though tinged with a shadow that was rarely spoken of—a presence hanging over us. Another doctor friend remarked, "These are your golden days. Cherish them."

This was also a time of shift in, and restlessness about, our church home. Both Harold and I had grown up in the Plymouth Brethren. In fact, my great-great-grandfather, a hymn-writer, had been one of the movement's founders. There was a strong emphasis on the Bible and on prayer.

Harold came to believe that the prayers of our friends were beginning to have an effect, that God was using them to heal him. People brought him books about faith and healing. But the doctor told me to "get our affairs in order," in effect propelling me into a double role—wanting with all my heart and soul to believe that God could heal my husband, and preparing myself to be a widow.

And in the end, I was.

"Rinsed with Gold, Endless, Walking the Fields"

These Wangerin letters, these very personal stories about an ongoing life with cancer and the threat of further pain and diminishment, are interspersed with meditations that move away from the writer's own experience into the wider world of mortality, of grief, of outrage, of learning to cope, and of the celebration of living. The book's second meditation consists wholly of a poem by our mutual friend Robert Siegel, "Rinsed with Gold, Endless, Walking the Fields," that encompasses a blissful vision of natural life with all its sensual beauty. As if to say, this too is part of mortality. And it is glorious.

One, more private, letter was written to a student of his at Valparaiso University in Indiana, where he continued to teach, an oxygen tank trailing behind him in his classes. Teaching and interaction with students invigorated him, gave him the sense that this meaningful work meant more than just a way of filling in the life yet available to him. He was open with them about his disease, hoping that they would grow less intimidated by it, and by its object.

⬦

Cancer infects its targets in ways that are universal, yet unique to the individual. Our responses differ. This is Walt Wangerin's story, and his wife's. Not mine. But because we are joined in our humanity and in longtime friendship, that splendid relationship includes our mortality. The Bible's words to Job and Walt, and now to me, are "Set your house in order, for you shall die." When it comes at us bluntly, like that, we realize its inescapability. It is a rude and disruptive message. Everything that makes up our rich, orderly, purposeful lives is tilted at a scary angle.

We are sliding off the shelf of living into . . . what? All we have to look forward to—some future immortal state—is metaphorical, beyond our earthbound reality to visualize. The future existence, even for people of profound Christian faith, is a big question mark.

And we seldom feel ready. We have books to write, vacations to take, continents to explore, ministries to sustain. Even with life insurance policies and medical insurance, death before old age has never been our plan at all. We long to see our children happily married, carrying on our family traditions, our faith.

OK, let me get even more personal. Several years ago, after months of belly pain and after the failure of all the medical and pharmacological suggestions from my family doctor, I went into the clinic for a colonoscopy, not nearly as unpleasant a procedure as many anticipate. It was followed by X-rays and scans. Something suspicious showed up, "somewhere between the size of a tennis ball and a marble." "A Ping-Pong ball?" I suggested. OK, a Ping-Pong ball. I determined to hit it across the net with my paddle.

Weeks of further tests and procedures followed and it was finally determined that my pain was caused by scar tissue from diverticulitis. A section of my colon infected with these little symptoms common to the aged was surgically removed. Sighs of relief and gratitude followed. My ordinary life resumed. But no life is ever really "ordinary," ordered, or predictable.

Against his will, but in accordance with the increasing weakness of the effects of radiation therapy, Walt grows snappish, impatient. He acknowledges grudgingly but apologetically that this is not Christ-like—Christ, who treated his friends and opponents with forbearance. He also reaches the conclusion that being disagreeable because of feeling lousy may take more effort than keeping his peace. He asks, "Who tells me that a terminal sickness gives me the right to be a churl?"

Self-examination is often how we learn to come to terms with difficulties bigger than we are. It is a kind of wrestling match with our feelings and beliefs. We *know* what the right attitude is, the right response, but when we feel and voice something different, the wholesome response is to ask *why*. What prompted us to display resentment? In this, Walter Wangerin becomes not only our case study, but also our exemplar. Such ruthless self-examination is not often made public; in this narrative it becomes a very honest confessional indeed.

He tells a story. A true one, about his interaction with his grandson Noah. They are tent camping in the woods—just the two of them. They come upon the rotting body of a deer, a gruesome sight that provokes a series of questions from the five-year-old. There are maggots, and a terrible stench. Noah asks: "What was the deer?" What he means is, "What am I seeing? What is going on here?" The strange concept of dying leads him to ask next, "Can a Papa die?"

And so this young one is first introduced to the ultimate condition of humanity, which is bodily mortality. Perhaps for the next question, about immortality, he will also find an answer from his grandfather.

〜⦿⦿〜

In Letter #6, our friend with cancer introduces the dynamic that shifts and strengthens between husband and wife when mortal illness strikes. Thanne, Walt's wife, a strong and steady woman already, now has to become the CEO of this business of Doctors & Dying, Inc. As they make decisions, she has to remind him of things like the high price of insurance and medical costs, practicalities that seem like insults to one already debilitated, for whom the condition of mind and body seem preeminent.

I remember a similar dissonance when Harold was so weakened that he'd forget or ignore things. I grew irritated when he didn't remember to take his medications on time. Or left uneaten the small, simple meals I'd prepared, hewing to a careful diet. My own level of anxiety and my burdens were already heavy. I became the family supervisor with a steep learning curve to achieve. Remembering to take a pill before a meal seemed like a simple thing. How careless it seemed to ignore it! And of course the guilt that followed my mild scoldings was redoubled, even after my asking for and gaining my husband's unstinting forgiveness.

The Experience of Pain

In Letter #8, Walt confesses what his conclusions are about pain—that he *contains* it. Someone else's pain is almost impossible to experience. And even for his own pangs his search for descriptive words is labored. He has nothing to compare pain to, but here he attempts a report:

> The deep, subterranean achings [have] returned. It grew into an interior battering hard enough to sometimes take my breath away. . . . I can't describe it as sharp. Nor as a burning pain. Nor rashlike nor stinging nor biting nor cutting. Nothing caustic. Not nausea. . . . In my skull. Behind my eyes. . . . And always, morning to night, in the dead center of my chest.

And later, "Groaning helps. . . . Transforming the pain into complete sentences."

This man knows how to tell a story. He doesn't rush it. The details arrive singly, one by one so that he knows we are following him closely. The descriptions and his inferences sink in, and our minds' eyes form the scenes, the settings. The dialog's natural speech patterns draw us into the conversation. We become participants, which, in Walt's telling, is always a benediction.

Sometimes the stories are about someone else's cancer, which he as a pastor is privileged to witness and accompany. This companionship adds a dimension to his own experience. He believes he is joining the large community of the afflicted and affected—a condition so universal it needs particulars to illustrate it. In this life with cancer he admits, "I'm finding my way, my friends—as much by writing this letter as by my more private, diffuse contemplations."

—◦◦◦—

In Letter #9 the anticipated result of chemo happens: "I've lost my hair. Almost all my hair . . . Naked as a baby rat." But then he compares this losing with the deliberate act of priestly tonsure and its leveling effect—"No hair, no individuality." He is now one in the company of the diseased, of basic, ongoing human need. As ever, he looks for and finds meaning in these things. The breathlessness when climbing stairs and the coughing it causes when his lung capacity is reduced is a constant reminder of the reduced capacity of that which sustains life. He's still tending his garden, with its deep reward of fruitfulness—his vegetables, and his strawberries in particular, bring him such a delicious sense of involvement in developing life. But for how long?

Time is heavy on his mind. He has a year of teaching ahead, the classroom instruction and mentoring that bring him joy and the fruitfulness that comes in the form of students who come alive under his leadership. As critical medical emergencies arise, a blood clot, surgery, more scans, increasing weakness, he grows more acutely aware that his planned academic life is liable to fall apart, ragged and unpredictable. Time is not on his side.

He is told by the oncological authorities, "This cancer doesn't go away. This cancer will kill you, unless something like pneumonia kills you first. Get used to it. Live your life with this in mind."

As he reflects on time, he wonders about the books he's been planning to write. "It makes a difference, choosing between what I want to do and what I need to do. Some things *must* be written before I die."

But in Letter #12, he suddenly realizes that with this series of letters he's "writing a book!" And that these deeply intimate communications of his may have the potential to speak more widely to the human race about the way this serious disease invades not just the body but "all the rest of me: my character, personality, faith, morality."

More recently, I have been remembering times spent together with Walt at Laity Lodge, a retreat in the Texas Hill Country where we in the Chrysostom Society have met annually for many years. A founding member of this group of Christian writers, Walt had continued to faithfully make the long flight and long drive to this wonderfully remote site.

Though looking gaunt and ravaged, he was still an arresting and restless presence, walking the grounds in the wind and rain of February, his oxygen tank following him like an obedient puppy. He was as engaged and engaging as ever. And Thanne, of course, was with him.

That Walt had felt impelled to join us again—that he was still part of our lives and we of his for the time being—was hugely significant. This group of friends that has stayed constant and in touch for over a quarter of a century has borne and continues to bear witness, as *Letters from the Land of Cancer* does, to the enduring power of a common aim of writing that speaks within and beyond the community of faith.

Weaving a World: Children, Memory, and the Story Experience

Sara R. Danger

Swallowing the Golden Stone (2001)

and Selected Works for Children

IN MY FIRST YEAR as a Lilly Postdoctoral Fellow at Valparaiso University, I visited the office of Professor Wangerin, writer-in-residence and Jochum Professor. I had come to ask the writer to visit my class on children's literature. A bearded man clad in rubber knee-high boots, jeans, and flannel shirt met me at the door. Once inside, he turned the conversation; he had some questions for *me*: Did I write regularly, and if so, why did I write? As a teacher, what did I require of my students? Most importantly, he wanted to know what I would be asking students to read in the course. I replied that we would be taking a historical and cultural approach, looking closely at landmark children's genres and considering aesthetic movements and cultural ideas associated with childhood.

We would start with chapbooks, the *New England Primer*, fairy tales, fantasy, literary realism, etc. He stopped me. "Fairy tales," he said, "what versions will you read?" When I told him we would start with stories by Perrault and the Grimm brothers, he nodded, "Good, good." His fear, he claimed, was the Disneyfication of the fairy tale. Disney had removed their large existential questions, he contended, watering them down, contorting them to fit one generic plotline of "I'm okay; you're okay" and "material things give life meaning." What the child needs, he insisted, were tales, such as "The Little Mermaid" by Hans Christian Andersen, which offered real portraits of tribulation and loss. Andersen's mermaid gives up her voice, her family, and her selfhood in her quest to acquire a human soul, whereas in the Disney version, she seeks the material goods of the human world and a man to love.

I left this first meeting puzzled. While I recognized problems implicit in Disney's storytelling, I took issue with the *grim* Grimm stories and *macabre* Andersen tales that Wangerin celebrated. While shopping markets under the sea offer no substitute for spiritual salvation, what do children gain from graphically violent tales, such as the Grimms' "Hansel and Gretel"? How are young readers to interpret child protagonists facing off against the witch-like cruelty of a stepmother followed by a real witch who tries to burn them alive? Protagonists may prove plucky—Hansel and Gretel's know-how with breadcrumbs and reverse psychology with witches, after all, saves the day—but the graphic angst and violence of these stories threatens to engulf readers.

Leaving Wangerin's office that day, I mulled over these concerns, concerns which stemmed from my scholarship on literature for children. In my graduate study of nineteenth-century British literature, I became fascinated by the era called the Golden Age of Children's Literature. This period between 1860 and 1880 marked an upswing in texts written for and about children. Artists such as Mark Twain, Lewis Carroll, Louisa May Alcott, Christina Rossetti, and Beatrix Potter banished didactic goody-two-shoes tales and gave voice to new imaginative genres. Their texts, moreover, could be interpreted as vital artifacts (holders and transmitters) of the ways that their culture valued and understood children. And the values and ideas endorsed were often fraught with paradox. Narratives that seemed to celebrate children's innocence contained messages that also undercut or threatened this ideal. Carroll's *Alice's Adventures in Wonderland*, for instance, can be read as a rompish exposé on childish naïveté; Alice hasn't learned her lessons well and she exists in an uncanny space familiar to children (i.e., their bodies and minds don't quite fit the spaces and rules of the adult world). More troubling, though, is that Alice's body literally *becomes* the site of her adventures—as she ingests various substances that make her grow larger and smaller. While Carroll would famously protest that

his story for and about Alice Liddell "wasn't meant to
teach anything at all," one had to ask what kinds of ideas
and values did Alice and her adventures promote about
girlhood? By extension, what notions of gender, race, and
class did boys' adventure tales by Kipling and H. Rider
Haggard instill? And what effect did the violence of
many fairy tales have on young readers, readers dealing
with their own sense of powerlessness, voicelessness, and
confusion—traits nearly all children share, whether born
in 1881 or 2008?

The further I investigated, the more children's
literature seemed less pure entertainment and more a
crucible through which language and power converge
in shaping children's understandings of self, other,
and the world. As Jacqueline Rose in *The Case of Peter
Pan* asserts, the power dynamic of much literature for
children is one-directional; it "sets up a world in which
the adult comes first (author, maker, giver) and the child
comes after (reader, producer, receiver)." As a result,
children's literature offers a vehicle through which
adults imaginatively work out their own desires and
ideas through the figure of the child. Jack Zipes similarly
argues that fairy tales, while imbued with the magic of
story, ultimately socialize child readers by endorsing
conservative gender and class behaviors.

While these perspectives offer a persuasive lens for
reconsidering adult desires encoded within children's
literature, I wondered if they become a self-fulfilling

prophecy. After all, as Marah Gubar argues: "The mere act of describing young people as voiceless can itself help *render* them voiceless." Increasingly, I wondered what children think of the stories written for them. Was Alice disturbing for some readers and pure farce for others? Was Tom Sawyer an endorsement of American male independence or a more gender-neutral portrait of active childhood? Entirely absent from most criticism of children's literature is *children's agency* as thinkers, artists, storytellers, and readers. Thus, I was left wondering what kind of stories did children tell, reappropriate, or seek to inhabit.

Naming the Wild Things

These questions took on new relevance after I became a parent. What the scholar sought to understand, the parent would learn differently. And what the parent discovered brought her back to Wangerin's theory that children need stories with real complexity and depth. As he contends in *Swallowing the Golden Stone*, "because children are already experts in difficulty," they need narratives that help them name "mortal anxiety so that they *can* attend to it . . . without being overwhelmed." Just a year after my first meeting with Wangerin, my four-year-old daughter would prove the truth of this sentiment.

One night, after returning home from teaching a

full slate of courses and attending an evening lecture, I headed for my daughter's bedroom in anticipation of our nightly ritual, which consisted of me sitting beside her sleeping form, offering a whispered prayer, and finally a benediction—a cross traced softly with fingers to forehead and a kiss on warm cheek. That night, however, I was unable to push open her door. Gently, I squeezed through the small opening and found that the blockage was not a misplaced toy, but rather my daughter, fast asleep behind her door. As I tried to carry her back to her bed, she awakened and protested shrilly, "No, no, no!"

In the moments that followed, I learned that earlier that day she had passed by her father watching television and she had seen news footage of war. The fleeting images had left their mark; she described bullets raining from helicopters onto city streets, people scurrying and screaming below. These images, which had haunted her all day, became all-consuming at bedtime. Now, though, the images of helicopters killing people were making their way down our quiet city street. In response, all she could do was move her body, blankets, and pillow to her doorway. That way, she told herself, if gun-toting soldiers should enter our home, her body would serve as a blockade. Her logic (rather, her story) ran thus: since the world outside no longer promised safety, she would use her own anatomy to protect the safe spaces she knew best—her bed, her room, her home.

Maia's fears so haunted her that for several nights I found her asleep behind her door, guarding it, in case an army truck should ramble down our street or rockets be aimed at her bed. During the late-night conversations that ensued, I stroked my daughter's hair and searched for words. Instead of having answers, I found myself suffering with her. She had entered a new reality; she had witnessed deep, systematic evil. "Why would people shoot guns at other people?" she asked. "Has this kind of thing ever happened before? Will someone start a war here? Why does God let people kill people?"

In these late-night conversations, our relationship shifted. I was no longer the one who blessed, soothed, and protected. Rather, I was put in the difficult position of trying to protectively love our tiny person while acknowledging the horrendous things of which humans are capable. On those nights, I became my daughter's companion in suffering, face to face with what Kjerstin Kauffman describes as

> a kind of terror implicit in parenting . . . a terror involving one's spirituality, recognizing that one is responsible, not just for someone's physical creation, but for their soul. We bring our children into a world where there are moral dangers, and where it can become clear in an instant that we do not know what we thought we did. The strongest moral convictions are open to reevaluation in light of the love one feels for one's child.

Indeed, many of my former "convictions"—moral, theological, and literary—were impacted by her nighttime vigils. All that I thought I had known about the relationship of language to power was open to question. I—the parent, the one with experience, the one who sought to protect—had little to offer by way of words and explanations. My attempts to explain God's presence amidst Maia's fears didn't stop her from moving all of her bedding to block her door night after night. Instead, she clung to her own stories of possible terror and laid her body out as the only barrier to evil she could imagine.

My child, as it turns out, taught me just as much as, if not more than, scholars had about what children need from stories. Her reactions proved what Bruno Bettelheim argued: "The child is subject to desperate feelings of loneliness and isolation, and [she] often experiences mortal anxiety." Furthermore, my failure to find words to comfort my child proved one of Wangerin's central contentions: no factual response, no explanation ever satisfactorily addresses children's "desperate feelings." Instead, fiction alone has the unique ability to name and companion the child through inexpressible trials. Because stories have the power to "acknowledg[e] and nam[e] the difficulties which children [have] only callowly *sensed* before, the plots of . . . stories can carry the child *through* difficulty toward a blessed, credible conclusion. And such conclusions to plots are, as you know, solutions to problems, now discovered not in rational explanations, but in experience." The understanding gained from story, Wangerin argues, is multifaceted and vicarious, not only impacting one's intellect but also providing a "'shaping' experience" more formative to a "person's sense of truth and of self than plain teaching." This experience "involves the whole of the [listener]; her calculating mind, all her senses (in the cauldron of her imagination), her affective heart and emotions, her moral judgments, her body in motion and laughter and fearful anticipations." By involving the whole reader, all of our senses, stories may help us navigate tribulations, enabling us to experience them intimately, emotively, yet safely at a distance.

What separates Wangerin's accounts of children's literature from those of other artists is his multi-perspectival approach, which illuminates the various ways by which children and adults (as artists, tellers, responders, and readers) participate in and give shape to the story experience. When discussing the power of fairy tales, for instance, Wangerin admits that as an adult he interprets fairy tales as "an entertaining escape from the problems of the real world"; as such, he "maintain[s] an analytical control over them; I read them. I interpret them; they don't interpret me." In his accompanying memories from childhood, however, he attributes to these tales a far different meaning: "As a child, I felt the tale; I sank inside it; I lived its composed experience from 'Once upon a time' to 'happily ever after.' I *lived* the solution to which the tale had walked me." In his essay, "To Weave a World," he places us inside his viewpoint as a five-year-old child who struggled to make sense of a parent's duplicitous behavior, which, in turn, led him to embrace the story of Snow White. He vividly recounts how entering the safe spaces of its fairy tale "world resolved my own most troubled world." Later, when discussing children's need for stories to interpret unexplainable evil, he reconstructs his own reasons for turning to storytelling as a boy. In elementary school, his first confrontations with bullying meant that

> Evil had entered my life. The shards and pieces of evil, miserably disconnected. Evil which, should it invade the consoling home, could destroy those dearest to me. . . . Ah, but I could—this nascent story-teller could—invoke fantasy to "story" it! And I did: I embodied formless evil in a figure, the robber, and I wrote into my story . . . contingent rules of action, by which rules the major character . . . (that was me, of course) could find some advantage over evil after all.

By giving voice to "the thickets of difficulty" defining his own childhood, Wangerin reconnects readers with our past trials and yearnings. And his narratives of childhood remind us of the multivalent power of stories—to heal, to perpetuate lies, to name truths, to please, to instruct; this power holds true for adults and children, though we may experience and interpret stories differently.

Evidence of this layered influence is demonstrated by Wangerin's praise for Maurice Sendak, the author to whom *Swallowing the Golden Stone* is dedicated. Even though he discovered Sendak after his own childhood had passed, as a college student and fledgling writer, he recalls that *Where the Wild Things Are*

> straightway seduced my soul by its deep familiarity and then stunned me by getting the childhood experience (*my* childhood experience) so right as to finish things unfinished before. . . . Here was a tale of fright and fight *with* a teller who knew my secrets, who was willing to confront the truth, and who danced like the piper in front of me, assuring me of safe endings. Sendak accomplished "presence" by the tone of his voice and the mood of his line. And I, the child and the writer, followed to the finish.

As he articulates his adult need for a narrative to name the unutterable realities of childhood and provide "safe endings," Wangerin presents us with another way of viewing not just stories, but also childhood and the human experience. From these vacillating yet interwoven perspectives, *Swallowing the Golden Stone* merges concepts typically held in binary tension, such as stories and truth, adulthood and childhood, writer and reader. As a result, these terms reemerge as categories that are not mutually exclusive but rather vitally interconnected, as part of the continuum of the human experience.

Getting It Right: "Speaking Truth in Love"

In Wangerin's stories, the binaries of extreme darkness and extreme goodness coexist. His works give voice to the "impossible complexities" of a child's existence *and* the extreme goodness of selfless love. On one side of the spectrum, Wangerin's tales "companion" children through real difficulty and suffering. The protagonist in *Branta and the Golden Stone* lives alone at the end of the earth having inherited endless loneliness and the sins of her father. In *Lily*, readers confront the reality of death with the protagonist, Lily, as her two sisters, Bean Plant and Marigold, and finally, Lily herself, fall prey to the fatal kiss of winter. While spring and new life provide the coda, the depiction of each sister's death absorbs the reader in grief. These tales and others make good on Wangerin's promise that his stories for children will not "sugarcoat" or "condescend"; they will not objectify children and their struggles, but rather they "companion" them through relatable struggles and fears.

Suffering, however, is never the end of the story. In a "world more hungry than whole," Wangerin's narratives reassure us of the "blessings" that abound. In nearly all of Wangerin's tales, sacrificial love becomes the anchor that promises "health and wholeness" to humanity. The picture book *The Bedtime Rhyme*, while expressing the child's potential nighttime fears, offers a more profound exploration of parental love. The maternal narrator promises to ward off all potential dangers—including robbers, monsters, and shadows—proclaiming her boundless love for the one she seeks to protect:

> Are you my strongest?
> Are you my smartest?
> Are you my baby true?
> . . .
> How much, my honeydew?
> How much do I love you?
> Lay down your head
> Sweet Gingerbread
> And listen: I'll tell you . . .

As the parent insists, she will follow her child anywhere, and her love knows no bounds. Yet, she also admits that: "Faster than I am / And higher than stars, / Stronger than you are / In both of your arms / . . . and best for safekeeping is God." The parent's boundless love points to a source deeper than itself: "God loves you even better than I." Though the act of motherly love might be commonplace, such offerings establish Wangerin's contention that the artist "must make public these blessings for the many." In his moving story *I Am My Grandpa's Enkelin*, the narrative explores the intergenerational love between grandfather and granddaughter. As the grandfather teaches his granddaughter the work and ways of farm life, searches patiently for her when she is lost in the cornfield, and tells her stories at night under the moon, he repeatedly sings to her a German lullaby about how she "abides in his heart" and is "always on his mind." After her grandfather's death, the now-grown granddaughter translates the full lyrics of his lullaby and discovers a deeper lesson. Even after his death sends her plummeting into despair, she learns from his lyrics that his love for her, too, bordered on inexpressible pain. Rather than sadness, this discovery points to a revelation through which she learns the true measure of profound love and faith.

Just as poignantly, Wangerin's *In the Beginning There Was No Sky* offers a stunning portrait of the Creator's love for creation. Retelling the creation story as it centers on the intimate, anticipatory making of a "clay-child," Wangerin depicts a profoundly relational and loving portrait of God and Creator, which culminates in the Creator kissing breath into the child, giving it life. As the narrator describes,

> the great Creator was crying. . . . Tears were falling from his eyes upon the face of his clay-child, and God was washing that face with his hands and his tears, so that there were two faces shining the same kind of light, one above the other.
>
> No, God was not sad. Neither was he hurt.
>
> God was crying because he loved this child so much. He was weeping for joy at the birth of a beautiful person.

Here and elsewhere, Wangerin's language invites readers to inhabit points of view not our own (even that of the Creator!). In this manner, stories are not just houses built out of piles of truth by tellers of tales; rather, they become "houses" through which readers navigate different spaces and vantage points of the human experience. As such, Wangerin's stories offer children the best of what imaginative literature offers: the development of a reader's moral imagination and empathy. Wangerin's stories invite us to see the world as a beautiful, inquisitive plant in *Lily*; as a troubled, lonely girl in *Branta*; and as a loving, weeping Creator in *No Sky*. In doing so, his fiction achieves the moral significance that Martha Nussbaum attributes to imaginative fiction. As she asserts, "literary imagining both inspires intense concern with the fate of characters and defines those characters as containing a rich inner life, not all of which is open to view; in the process, the reader learns to have respect for the hidden contents of that inner world." Thus, stories like Wangerin's invite children to "wonder" about perspectives and realities other than their own; by so doing, readers develop habits of empathy, learning to "define the other person as spacious and deep, with qualitative differences from oneself and hidden places worthy of respect."

A powerful example of the ways that Wangerin's narratives engage readers' empathy is found in *Probity Jones and the Fear Not Angel*. In Wangerin's picture book, illustrated by Tim Ladwig, image and text work together and involve us in Probity's struggles and her encounter with the miraculous; we intimately come to "walk *with* her, as it were, but not yet with-*in* her."

In the first pages, we identify with the sidelined Probity; her fever stands between her longing to perform in the Christmas pageant and her mother "worn out from working, worn out from taking care of four children alone, worn out from being forever and ever poor." Her mother offers the rationale for why Probity should stay home—"'Baby . . . when I lost your daddy to sickness, I promised God I'd never lose another soul. I'm keeping the family whole, and you are staying home tonight.'" Thus, we learn that Probity and her mother's sufferings have a long history. Our empathy, which builds as Probity's sister chides her for losing her prized winter coat, escalates as we learn how it was taken from her. In word and picture, Probity appears defenseless and small as three bullies steal her jacket. In the image, we look down from above as her tiny, cocooned body appears vulnerable and alone within the long corridors of a city alley.

Pages later, the "Fear Not" angel appears, "tall as the night. She had wings wider than the dawn with feathers more silent than snow." The accompanying image invites us to look with Probity at the looming, ebony face of the angel. The angel's downcast eyes and slight, knowing smile ready us for her knowing kiss and her call to "Come . . . to the Christmas Pageant, of course." As she gathers Probity in her arms and they "crossed seas as deep as dreaming," she assures her: "'Fear not, Probity. God would never let you fall—and who else but God has invited you to the pageant." The angel shrouds Probity in her downy, expansive wings, her devoted gaze shielding Probity's anticipatory, expressive face.

In the final pages, readers observe the pageant's story of Christ's miraculous birth from Probity's miraculous perspective far above the stage, enveloped in the wings of an angel. As such, the story of God-made-man takes on new meaning. As readers witness this familiar story told by another disadvantaged, poor child born to a suffering mother and redeemed by God's miraculous grace, we, too, are changed by the encounter. Our vicarious encounter with the angel has given us, like Probity, "a piece of herself to keep forever and forevermore."

ENGAGING WITH METAPHORS: CHILDREN AND THE STORY EXPERIENCE

Throughout *Swallowing the Golden Stone*, Wangerin focuses on the metaphorical power of stories to convey participatory, imaginative truth and thereby deepen our understanding of self and other. And yet, as Wangerin argues, the "shaping" influence of a story belongs not to the teller alone. Rather, the audiences of art—in this case, children—are the ones who experience the story and determine its meaning. As he insists: "Each child can and will . . . choose the level of reality at which he or she shall experience the tale." Furthermore, according to Wangerin's "To Weave a World," the depth of this engagement takes many forms. Some readers may see a story as mere entertainment, a diversion from the everyday. Others might acknowledge the "truthfulness" of the tale. At a deeper level, a child may empathetically connect with the protagonist, the fictional not-me. At the very deepest level, the child's identification with the tale becomes so great that she truly and fully enters the reality of the story.

And the story a child chooses to inhabit can be surprising. As a goddaughter of a storyteller and inheritor of many books, my youngest daughter, Ingrid, relishes the ritual of choosing her own bedtime reading. At a young age, the book she most often selected surprised us; *Thistle* became her Wangerin story of choice. Even at the tender age of two and a half, Ingrid would plead with me to read her this shiny tome. I thought the book contained too much difficulty for one so young, so I suggested substitutes: "How about *The Bedtime Rhyme* or *Water Come Down*?" (two books by Wangerin with pleasing rhymes and messages about God's enduring love). I'd ask to no avail. Ingrid, book in chubby hand, insisted again and again, "No, this one." So we settled into our reading chair, and once again entered the story world of *Thistle* with its woodland people, quaint cottages, forest paths, and witches.

What begins as a tale of a simple man with simple work quickly becomes existentially dark—as the best fairy tales do. Just pages in, the conflict is introduced: the farmer/patriarch comes face-to-face with a thousand-eyed, giant potato named Pudge. Rather than continue his work harvesting potatoes, the farmer's work literally consumes him. Pudge eats the farmer and eventually his wife and children. The only hope for change comes in the form of a haggard Beldame. While her nose and cheek appear like sharp shears, she offers to help each child in turn if they would but kiss her. One could say that the children's pride gets in the way—hubris again. Oak thinks he is too strong to be kissed, and his sister Rose considers herself too beautiful. Yet, if the secret to saving your family entails kissing a hideous witch-like creature, the bind seems real. In the end, only the youngest child, Thistle—the smallest, weepiest, last-surviving, and weakest of all her family—survives.

When Thistle finally confronts the witch, she alone accepts the Beldame's request: she grants her a kiss. In response, the Beldame turns her tears into thorns, which become the armor that Thistle needs to defeat Pudge and get her family back.

Each time we would read the story, I was amazed by Ingrid's total immersion. When I asked her what she liked about the story, she responded first with gestures and leanings and later with words. I discovered that she found Pudge more funny than villainous. In her eyes, Pudge was less an existential threat and more symbolic of hunger—familiar, indiscriminate, crabby hunger.

"He's just so hungry," she would say, often followed by a laugh. Most of all, she patiently listened to the very long narrative because of the smallest weeping girl in the background. As she would say, pointing to the cover and again at the end, "That's me, the little one, and she has my cheeks." What I had interpreted as a narrative profuse with polysyllabic language that would stretch a ten-year-old's vocabulary—let alone a two-year-old's— she patiently enjoyed. She enjoyed the vivid language, its rhythm and cadence, as much as its meanings. A plot that I had perceived as too existentially dark (e.g., a man-eating giant potato, an entire family consumed, a lonely child, and a suspicious witch), Ingrid had viewed differently. She associated Pudge with unbridled hunger and Thistle with herself. Like Thistle, Ingrid was the youngest, most emotive member of our family, who saw herself as overlooked. She identified with Thistle's bravery and trust as well as her tears. Even in her small, helpless, weepy state, Thistle's compassion proved forceful enough to save herself and her entire family from their own prideful self-sufficiency.

Gifts from the Storyteller

Before I had read Wangerin's works, I heard Wangerin the storyteller. In January 2004, while visiting Valparaiso University's Chapel of the Resurrection for the first time, I watched intently as a bearded, robed man stepped forward to preach. Even before he began, his eyes searched the crowd. Though his lectionary text was from Isaiah 6:8—"Then I heard the voice of the Lord saying, 'Whom shall I send? And who will go for us?' And I said, 'Here am I. Send me!'"—he did not preach or pontificate; instead, he told a story of his days as a young pastor called to a church in Evansville, Indiana. He wove his story humbly, organically, retelling his first assumptions about Isaiah's calling and then relaying how a few youth in his congregation had caused him to reexamine this theology. As he spoke, he roamed, pacing back and forth within the vast chapel space. He chewed his lips, scowled, smiled, and looked up to the heavens. Row upon row of upturned, hushed faces, including mine, became enfolded in his story. He told us how he had wrongfully chided the young parishioners, rebuking them for behaving as hoodlums. As the story turned to confession, we learned that the hoodlums were just children, sufferers and survivors of the sins of their parents.

In his narrative of prideful perspective turned to grace, we saw the "speck of sin" limiting our vision and obscuring our perception of the need of restoration. Such a speck had distracted me as I sat down that day to worship. On campus that weekend for the Lilly Postdoctoral Fellowship interview weekend, I became consumed with my role as "interviewee." I was weighted down by anxiety and doubt. Yet, as his story absorbed me in the

rhythms of pride, sin, confession, forgiveness, and restoration, I experienced a radical reorientation of mind,
heart, and body. My pulse returned to normal, my presence in worship returned, my confession became real,
and anchors of faith and vocation were restored.

Before sitting down to the storyteller's tale, I had
spent more than ten years studying English literature;
in those years, I had thought deeply about the aesthetic
shape and cultural resonance of stories. Experiencing
Wangerin's story that day, however, provided me with a
new perspective on the magnetic pull and resonance of
a story well told; it was the first time since childhood
that an oral storyteller had so completely involved me
in story.

Today, whenever Wangerin visits my classes or
preaches, I relish the opportunity to observe his
storytelling and its transformational effects. By now, I
have heard several of his narratives multiple times, and
yet, they are never the same. While the central structure
remains intact (what Wangerin calls the "houseness"
of the story), each time, he adds new details, living
tendrils and sprouting leaves that grant new shape to
the story's resonance. As his voice draws us in, I have
watched roomfuls of children and adults fall silent.
Restless, shifting, cell-phone-checking bodies become
subdued and entranced as the storyteller moves them
inside the house of his tale. In the process, Wangerin
takes stories out of the province of the scholar—one

who austerely judges, appropriates, and labels. Instead, his stories are generative, experiential, and relational. More than cultural myths that damage and lie, stories, well told and with proper grounding in the real, are the building blocks of our humanity. As such, they offer a profound source for compassion and empathy, renewal and understanding. No longer a skeptic and critic of stories, like many Wangerin fans, I am now a seeker and believer.

Afterword

Philip Yancey

I HAVE THE ADVANTAGE OF reviewing other contributors' chapters (though not the Foreword) before
writing my own reflections on Walter Wangerin Jr.
As I do so, it strikes me that all of these accomplished
writers have taken a detour. After volunteering to survey
the work of a colleague they both love and admire, they
ended up describing Wangerin's impact on their own
lives and work.

Eugene Peterson, sometimes called "the pastor's
pastor," whose own memoir is titled simply, *The Pastor*,
credits Wangerin's very first book with helping to
clarify his understanding and practice of the life of a
pastor. The book, a guide to Peterson for nearly forty
years, is a fantasy novel based loosely on a tale from

Geoffrey Chaucer. It stars a rooster and a basilisk,
along with such supporting characters as a rat, a fox,
a toad, and a melancholy dog. Peterson explains that
this unlikely tale diagnoses what's wrong with modern
culture, infected as it is by covert evils that also threaten
to undermine the Christian community. Wangerin's
genre of "theological fiction" pulled Peterson away
from an obsession with "relevance" and in the process
restored his pastoral imagination. (You'll not find that
genre in any bookstore, by the way: Amazon places *Dun
Cow* in the category of Metaphysical and Visionary
Fantasy.)

   Jim Schaap, himself a master storyteller, tackles the
more realistic stories, true encounters from Wangerin's
career that formed the basis for his fictionalized
chronicles of grace. Schaap correctly identifies the
central tension of Wangerin's writing, the tug between
artist and sermonizer. Every writer of faith lives with
that tension, and Schaap examines how well Wangerin
follows his own rules of writing integrity before asking
whether he himself has honored those rules. He looks to
the model of *Miz Lil and the Chronicles of Grace* as "by
far the most memorable text in my writing education."

   Diane Glancy, a Native American, dissects
Wangerin's novel *The Crying for a Vision*, set among
the Lakota tribe before the coming of Europeans
and the Christian religion. She ranks it among the
books most central in expressing the clash that arises

between European and native, Christian faith and tradition. While doing research for the novel, Wangerin participated in the Sun Dance ritual of the Lakota. His insights into the "common grace" evident in the Lakota myths helped her resolve the tension between two cultures and pointed her back toward faith.

Bringing together three of Wangerin's disparate works, Matthew Dickerson takes the autobiographical approach even further. In the three—a sequel to *Dun Cow*, a Greek myth embodied in the life of a modern pastor, and a medieval romance—Dickerson finds the same story told three ways. It is, in fact, Wangerin's own story, of Lutheran guilt and desolation swallowed up in the mercy and forgiveness of God. By projecting himself in his work, Wangerin, "the protagonist who must fall to the very bottom, and then fall even further," has presented a *Pilgrim's Progress* in which every pilgrim can find radical authenticity as well as radical hope.

Most poignantly, Luci Shaw reflects on *Letters from the Land of Cancer*. Here the connection between writer and reader becomes most intimate, for Luci also battled the disease, losing her husband to the very same type of cancer that has afflicted Wangerin since 2006. It is a small book by Wangerin standards, but one that strips away any need for fantasy or other artistic device. Much like *A Grief Observed* by C. S. Lewis, *Letters* is trenchant, and raw. Whatever Wangerin has hoped or despaired, believed or doubted, loved or lost, is put to the test in his decade-long struggle, an ordeal that Luci Shaw knows as well as anyone.

The novelist Walker Percy once remarked that fiction does not tell us something we do not know; it tells us what we know but do not know that we know. The principle applies in varying degrees to all art. In each of the chapters written in tribute to Walter Wangerin Jr., the writers bring to the surface universal themes and insights that have lain buried but, once exhumed, seem inescapable: "Yes, at last I see." Sara Danger's remarkable chapter on Wangerin's children's literature may illustrate that best. Her encounter with the author and his work helped transform her understanding of what children's stories can achieve, while giving us a sharp glimpse of the author himself.

⚬≈≈⚬

The books discussed, which give a sense of Wangerin's range, represent a mere sampling of his work. He has written thirteen children's books, as well as books about prayer, and marriage, and grief, and childhood, and he has experimented with poetry, sermons, a mass, and meditations on Christmas and Easter and the Passion—oh yes, and also narrative retellings of Jesus, Paul, and the entire Bible. In his spare time he has taught literature, homiletics, and theology, has pastored a church, has reared two birth and two adopted children, and has traveled widely as a speaker.

In fact, I first encountered Walt as a speaker, at a conference in which we both participated. A slender man with a handsome, angular face and a shock of dark hair, he stalked the stage like a Shakespearean actor. I thought of the accounts of Charles Dickens sitting onstage in the great halls of England reading his stories to a mesmerized audience—yet Wangerin was neither reading nor sitting. He was performing in the purest sense of the word, weaving stories and concepts together in erudite prose, directing our minds and emotions much as a conductor directs an orchestra's sounds, now meditative and melodic, now electrifying and bombastic.

We got to know each other mainly through the Chrysostom Society, a group comprising twenty or so writers of faith, including all the contributors to this volume, except one guest. Walt usually sat quietly on the margins, stroking his then-shaven chin while observing with piercing blue eyes everything around him. He rarely showed emotion, and when he spoke, he acted as a peacemaker, calming the heated arguments that sometimes emerged from the gaggle of writers. As a public speaker, however, he took on a new persona, passionate and dramatic. He saw himself in the line of medieval bards or scops who conveyed truth lyrically, and indeed he carried on that tradition both in speaking and writing.

A few years before, he had published *The Book of the Dun Cow*. At the time he was trying to support his family on the meager salary provided by his predominantly African American church, and his days were filled with counseling, parenting, social work, and the many tasks of an inner-city pastor. To his surprise, more than anyone's, his first book won the National Book Award in the "Science Fiction" category, a prestigious award that propelled him into the exalted company of other winners that year: Douglas Hofstadter's *Gödel, Escher, Bach*, Barbara Tuchman's *A Distant Mirror*, Henry Kissinger's *White House Years*, Peter Matthiessen's *The Snow Leopard*, Tom Wolfe's *The Right Stuff*, John Irving's *The World According to Garp*, William Styron's *Sophie's Choice*, Madeleine L'Engle's *A Swiftly Tilting Planet*.

Walt and I became fast friends. I had been working in publishing for more than a decade, and he had many questions about the arcane world of editors, agents, and marketing. He wanted only to write, and had just resigned from the church in order to devote himself to the craft full-time. I answered dozens of letters of anguish about the pressure from publishers to modify his style. Editors drove him crazy. They urged him to streamline his "heightened prose" and adopt a more pragmatic tone, shifting away from his natural tendency toward indirection. Walt would listen to their advice, agonize for weeks, and ultimately decide to ignore it.

Jim Schaap's chapter spells out the Wangerin rules of writing integrity. No doubt, staying true to those rules cost Walt a broader readership. For example, his *As for Me and My House* contains more helpful advice than a dozen books on "Ten Steps for a Better Marriage," yet he rightly refused to accommodate his natural style to the artificiality of self-help bromides. He chose to subsume some of his most powerful personal experiences into *The Orphean Passages*, knowing that many readers would miss the Greek myth's overtones. And in private conversations I heard from him chilling childhood stories that he declined to write because of the pain it would cause family members.

Walt knew he was swimming against the tide. He spoke of the "cool pragmatism" of modern literary taste. "Precision has become nearly a morality," he wrote me, referring to "the precisions of objective observation, analytic theologies, intellectual persuasions." He sought instead to draw the reader into another world, a suspension of disbelief carried more by music and lyricism than by sense and reason. "A writer hopes for the obedience of a good reader who says, 'I will enter this world a while, however different it is from my own more familiar expressions of truth.' The impressionist painters sought the same while yet the Academy was committed to a 'classical' aesthetic, unwilling to obey the new principles of the newer generation. But what would the world do without romantics?"

That last sentence may be the most telling. Walt is a true romantic, his sensibilities shaped more by prior centuries than by this one. Others, he said, "use the metaphor in service of intellectual comprehension. I *live* the metaphor. For some, speech is a medium. For me speech is a music."

Early on, I found myself acting as a kind of guide as Walt confronted the burgeoning evangelical subculture. A lifelong Lutheran, he was accustomed to careful exposition and liturgical worship. I remember when he first heard Tony Campolo speak. He marveled "that a man can be so loud, so funny, and so angry, all at the same time." Eventually Walt himself became a prophetic voice to many evangelicals, a popular speaker and frequent interview subject.

Once we spent a weekend evaluating each other's manuscripts. We took a break to hike the grounds of a conference center near Colorado Springs, and suddenly found ourselves strolling in a meadow where grazed a herd of Rocky Mountain sheep. We stopped walking so as not to scare them and stood in silence for a few minutes, watching. "Want to see a trick?" Walt whispered. "I can whistle at a frequency higher than the human ear can detect."

I looked at him skeptically. "And if I can't hear it, how will I know?"

"Watch those sheep," he said. "I'll start high, and then work down to a frequency you can hear." He pursed his lips and blew, and not a sound came out that I could detect. Instantly, though, the sheep halted their grazing and lifted their heads, newly alert. A few seconds later I heard his piercing whistle in a descending scale.

That image has stayed with me, for as I review the shelf full of books written by my friend, I realize that he both hears and speaks in unique ways. I learned to be gentle with my own editorial suggestions for Walt. "The horns of a snail retract at a touch," he once wrote me. He worries over his books as he worries over his children. They are, to him, sacred offerings, given in response to a prompting others do not perceive and sometimes do not understand.

———

In time, Walt began to question his pell-mell approach to writing. Due to the cancer, death stares him in the face every day. I last saw him bald from the chemo-therapy—"naked as a baby rat," in his words—wheezing and dragging behind him an oxygen tank as he walked me a few yards to my car. "My body is weak but my mind is fine," he assured me. Later, he confessed in a letter, "Most of my career I've been a breathless kid, rushing things to publication before they were really ready, and now I'm sorry about that. Too messy and too stupid." He has returned to some of his major works and made extensive revisions. He wants to clean up his legacy, with books that yield artistic pleasure as well as joy.

Lutheran theology centers on two great themes, the cross and grace, and these themes underlie all of Walt's work. As both a sermonizer and artist, with graduate degrees in theology and English, he has lived with the constant tension of how best to express those themes. As a pastor he found that *story* conveys truth most effectively and profoundly. As he told one interviewer, "While the intellect must be addressed in communicating Christian truth, it will not be truth for the hearer until the hearer is also touched deep within himself or herself. . . . Truth, as I understand it, has a capital T and is alive. It is Jesus Christ. Christ is the one the preacher knows by faith and wishes to communicate to others that they might experience his saving power. Here the preacher has the advantage! Nevertheless, the preacher must know the truths of human experience, too."

Although Walt has a mystical, otherworldly side, he has nevertheless lived in the mess of human experience. In academic days, he joined a protest movement that formed a breakaway seminary-in-exile. In his twenties, he led a church congregation with a different racial and social makeup than any he had known. He has chaired committee meetings, ministered to street people, nego-tiated a blended family, taught Bible and literature to cynical undergraduates. On a whim he bought a farm, where he spent many hours repairing fences, mowing grass, and building a writing retreat reachable only by a trek on wooden planks across muddy fields.

After the success of *The Book of the Dun Cow*, Wangerin was invited to speak on university campuses. He discovered that when he went as a pastor, the left-brained, conceptual approach failed to hold attention. Students assumed he was putting boundaries on reality, not imparting it. On the other hand, when he went as a storyteller, he could function as a kind of priest. "Tell us a story," they said, and sat down like children. By drawing on the mess of human experience, he could mediate the fear and bewilderment they felt about the adult world they would soon enter.

"If I go as a writer they assume that I've gone through all the torments, all the anguish a prophet should go through and, I mean, I've suffered. And not only have I suffered, but I've survived in order to write, and I've come to some sense of hope because writing is always putting disorder into order."

I recently came across one letter that Walt wrote me from Cameroon, Africa, in 1995. In his vivid prose, he described an appalling sight, of two black birds perched on the haunch of a donkey pecking at an open wound. The African driver of his car yearned for a gun to put the animal out of its misery. Three days later, returning down the same road, they saw the donkey now lying on the ground, with five birds, their beaks bloody red, pecking away at muscle tissue. Walt despised those birds, and pitied the poor donkey—until later he learned the truth. The birds were oxpeckers, born with crimson beaks. Far from hurting the beast, they were cleansing its wound of the maggots breeding there. They were, in fact, making it possible for the donkey to live.

Some have accused Wangerin's books of a tone of morosity. He writes of child abuse, and cancer, and a Book of Sorrows, and a cursed, murderous saint, and a deluded rooster, and a collapsed Native American culture, and the Passion of Jesus. He writes, in other words, of the reality of our fallen planet in all its brokenness. Yet Walt is also a Lutheran pastor. He writes to heal, that we might live. To put disorder into order.

Knowing the man and his story, including parts of it he has not yet written, I want to give him a kind of benediction. I want to say, "Walt, like Saint Julian, like the rooster Chauntecleer, you have been through the silent passage—a time when God was not speaking. You have plumbed the depths, falling to the very bottom. And there you have tasted grace. You have found The Story at the foundation of the universe, that by his wounds we are healed. And you have faithfully and artfully passed it on. Rest content, Walter, my friend. You have given us life."

Selected Bibliography

Listed below are resources that have been of use in the writing of this book. This is by no means a complete record of all the works and sources consulted but is intended to serve as a convenience for those who wish to further pursue an interest in Walter Wangerin Jr.'s, work and influence. It also includes the particular writers and fictions that are referenced in this collection.

1. CHAUNTECLEER AND THE PASTORAL
    IMAGINATION (EUGENE PETERSON)

Chaucer, Geoffrey. *Canterbury Tales*. A. C. Cawley, ed. London: Everyman's Library, 1958.

Dickinson, Emily. *The Poems of Emily Dickinson: Reading Edition*. Ralph W. Franklin, ed. Cambridge, MA: The Belknap Press-Harvard University Press, 1998.

Dillard, Annie. *Holy the Firm*. New York: Harper & Row, 1977.

Newbigin, Lesslie. *The Gospel in a Pluralist Society*. Grand Rapids, MI: Eerdmans, 1989.

Pound, Ezra. *Cantos*. In *The Old Poetries and the New*,

Richard Kostelanetz (University of Michigan Press, 1981), 48.

Wangerin Jr., Walter. *The Book of the Dun Cow.* New York: HarperCollins, 1978.

Wangerin Jr., Walter. *The Book of Sorrows.* New York: HarperCollins, 1985.

Wangerin Jr., Walter. *The Third Book of the Dun Cow: Peace at the Last.* New York: Diversion Publishing, 2013.

Rosenstock-Huessy, Eugen. In *Speech and Society: The Christian Linguistic Social Philosophy of Eugen Rosenstock-Huessy*, George Allen Morgan (Gainesville: University Press of Florida, 1987).

Rosenstock-Huessy, Eugen. In *The Cultivated Life: From Ceaseless Striving to Receiving Joy,* Susan S. Phillips, (Downers Grover, IL: InterVarsity Press, 2015).

Yancey, Philip. *The Question That Never Goes Away: Why?* Grand Rapids, MI: Zondervan, 2014.

2. Singing and Preaching: The Short Works (J. Schaap)

Lowell, James Russell. *A Fable for Critics.* New York: Putnam. First published 1848, anonymously.

Schaap, James Calvin and Phillip Yancey, eds. *More Than Words: Contemporary Writers on the Works That Shaped Them*. Ada, MI: Baker Books, 2002.

Wangerin Jr., Walter. *Miz Lil & the Chronicles of Grace*. Grand Rapids, MI: Zondervan, 2003.

Wangerin Jr., Walter. *Ragman and Other Cries of Faith: Revised and Updated with 11 New Stories*. New York: HarperSanFrancisco, 2004.

Wangerin Jr., Walter. *The Book of the Dun Cow*. New York: HarperOne, 2003.

3. THE SUN WITH BITES TAKEN OUT
   (D. GLANCY)

Erdoes, Richard. *Crying for a Dream: The World Through Native American Eyes*. Rochester, VT: Bear & Company, 1990.

Erdrich, Louise. *Love Medicine*. New York: Holt, Rinehart and Winston, 1984.

McComb, Marianna. *The Art of Reading*. https://selvesandbookshelves.wordpress.com/2012/04/22/wangerins-crying/

Momaday, Scott. *House Made of Dawn*. New York: Harper & Row, 1968.

Neihardt, John G. *Black Elk Speaks: Being the Life Story of a Holy Man of the Oglala Sioux*. Lincoln: University of Nebraska Press, 1961.

"Review of *The Crying for a Vision* by Walter Wangerin Jr." *Publisher's Weekly*, May 29, 2000.

Silko, Leslie Marmon. *Ceremony*. New York: Penguin, 1977.

Wangerin Jr., Walter. *The Crying for a Vision*. New York: Simon & Schuster, 1994.

Welch, James. *Winter in the Blood*. New York: Harper & Row, 1974.

4. PASSAGES OF FAITH
(M. DICKERSON)

Heard, Mark. Conversation with Pat Terry in *Hammers and Nails: The Life and Music of Mark Heard* (Dickerson, Matthew,). Chicago: Cornerstone Press, 2005.

Heard, Mark. Liner Notes, *Appalachian Melody*. Produced by Larry Norman. Solid Rock Records, 1979.

Tolkien, J. R. R. *Letters of J. R. R. Tolkien*, Humphrey Carpenter, ed. Boston: Houghton Mifflin, 1981.

Wangerin Jr., Walter. *The Book of Sorrows*. New York: HarperCollins, 1985.

Wangerin Jr., Walter. *Orphean Passages*. Grand Rapids, MI: Zondervan, 1986.

Wangerin Jr., Walter. *Saint Julian*. San Francisco: HarperCollins, 2003.

5. LETTERS FROM THE LAND OF CANCER
   (L. SHAW)

Wangerin Jr., Walter. *Letters from the Land of Cancer*. Grand Rapids, MI: Zondervan, 2010.

6. WEAVING A WORLD: CHILDREN, MEMORY, AND THE STORY EXPERIENCE (S. DANGER)

Gubar, Marah. "Risky Business: Talking about Children in Children's Literature Criticism." *Children's Literature Association Quarterly* 38 (2013): 450–57.

Kauffman, Kjerstin. "Broken Bell: Some Thoughts on Parenting and Poetry." *The Cresset* 79 (2016): 19–22.

Nussbaum, Martha. *Cultivating Humanity: A Classical Defense of Reform in Liberal Education*. Cambridge, MA: Harvard University Press, 1998.

Rose, Jacqueline. *The Case of Peter Pan, or The Impossibility of Children's Fiction*. Philadelphia, PA: University of Pennsylvania Press, 1993.

Wangerin Jr., Walter. *Thistle*. Minneapolis, MN: Augsburg Fortess, 1995.

Wangerin Jr., Walter. *Probity Jones and the Fear Not Angel*. Minneapolis, MN: Augsburg Fortress, 1996.

Wangerin Jr., Walter. *In the Beginning There Was No Sky*. Minneapolis, MN: Augsburg Fortress, 1997.

Wangerin Jr., Walter. *Swallowing the Golden Stone*. Minneapolis, MN: Augsburg Fortress, 2001.

Wangerin Jr., Walter. *I Am My Grandpa's Enkelin*. Brewster, MA: Paraclete Press, 2007.

Zipes, Jack. *Fairy Tales and the Art of Subversion*. London: Routledge, 1991.